DEVELOPING THE
WORKFORCE
OF YOU!

SAMUEL J. VARNER

DEVELOPING THE
WORKFORCE
OF YOU!

A GUIDE TO A HARMONIOUS WORK-LIFE AND SOUL

SAMUEL J. VARNER

Hunter Entertainment Network
Colorado Springs, Colorado

DEVELOPING THE WORKFORCE OF YOU!
Copyright © 2020 Samuel J. Varner
First Edition: December 2020

All rights reserved. No part of the book may be reproduced or transmitted in any form or by any means, electronic or mechanical, including photocopying, recording, or by an information storage and retrieval system without permission in writing from the publisher.

To order products, or for any other correspondence:

Hunter Entertainment Network
4164 Austin Bluffs Parkway, Suite 214
Colorado Springs, Colorado 80918
Tel. (253) 906-2160 – Fax: (253) 912-1667
E-mail: contact@hunter-ent-net.com
Or reach us on the internet: www.hunter-ent-net.com

"Offering God's Heart to a Dying World"

This book and all other Hunter Entertainment Network™, Hunter Heart Kids™, and Hunter Heart Publishing™ books are available at Christian bookstores and distributors worldwide.

Chief Editor: Deborah G. Hunter
Cover design by Phil Coles Independent Design
Logos & Layout Design: Exousia Marketing Group

ISBN: 9798578041952
For Worldwide Distribution, Printed in the United States of America.

DEDICATION

I dedicate this book to two people who have shaped me into the person I am today. The unabashed love of my grandmother, Louisiana Varner, who taught me that silence is more potent than a mouth full of words. It was her strength and willingness to persevere no matter what life threw at her that always reminds me never to give up and that life does get better.

I cannot forget my uncle Kenneth McFarlane who treated me more like a son. I miss them both tremendously, but I know that they are always with me. Even when times are tough, I always feel like they are with me. It is their love that still guides me, although they are not physically present with me any longer. The love and lessons I have learned from them empower me in times of sorrow, and I remember all the good times I shared with them both.

TABLE OF CONTENTS

Introduction 1
1. Do Your Job! 3
2. Come to Work on Time 5
3. Start on the Right Foot 9
4. Never Be Afraid to Ask Questions! 11
5. Maintain a Professional Tone at All Times, Regardless of the Medium 13
6. Proofread Your Work 17
7. Wash Your Hands...Literally! 19
8. Your Appearance 21
9. Don't Do Drugs on the Job 23
10. Your Reputation is the Most Significant Currency that You Have, Don't Become Devalued 25
11. Give Credit Where Credit is Due................................... 27
12. If You Don't Value Yourself, Why Should Anyone Else? 29
13. A Little Kindness Goes a Long Way 31
14. Privacy... Don't Expect Any.. 33
15. Use the Resources Around You..................................... 35
16. Use Office Supplies for Office Use Only...................... 37
17. If You Are an Introvert, You Can't Be At Work........... 39

18. Learn Another Language 41
19. You Only Get What You Put In 43
20. I Don't Receive the Praise I Should 45
21. Education, Education, Education 47
22. Time 49
23. Make Yourself Invaluable, But Within Reason 51
24. Burnout is Inevitable, But There are Ways to Manage It 53
25. NEVER Accept a Friend Request From a Supervisor & Most Colleagues 57
26. Faith... We All Need It 59
27. Leave the Office at the Office 61
28. Volunteer for Special Projects 63
29. Know Your Limit & Use Discretion 65
30. Clean Your Desk Regularly: An Unscheduled Absence Might Not Work in Your Favor 67
31. Always Remain Calm 69
32. Mentorship is Essential 71
33. Networking 73
34. If You Don't Ask For It, Don't Expect It 75
35. Don't Steal Your Colleague's Lunch 77
36. Revenge is a Dish Best Served Cold, But Sometimes, It's a Dish That Doesn't Need to Be Served at All 79
37. Respect the Religious Beliefs of Others 81
38. Never Fear Success, Embrace It 83

39. If You Can, Get Others to Do Some, Whole, or Part of Your Work for You, Then Do So.. 85

40. If You Tell Anyone in the Office Your Business, You Might as Well Have Told the Entire Office... 87

41. Don't Let Bad Situations Poison Your Soul 89

42. Every So Often, Dress Like You Are Going on An Interview.... 91

43. Ethical Behavior 93

44. Money Isn't Everything 95

45. Sometimes, I Feel Like I am Still in High School 97

46. It's Review Time, Put Your Game Face On 99

47. I Have a Last-Minute Meeting, and I Want to Make a Good Impression 101

48. If Your Supervisor is About to Jump Ship, Consider Doing the Same..103

49. Create Your Work Mantra..105

50. Never Stay Longer than Five Years with a Company if You Have Not Received a Promotion 107

51. A Job is A Lot Like a Relationship, It Starts Well and Can Go Downhill From There 109

52. I'm Getting Fired, All Hope is Not Lost 111

53. You Can't Make Everyone Happy, So Don't Even Try 113

54. My Colleagues Don't Like Me...115

55. Gossip is Not Necessarily a Bad Thing, but Always Beware of the Office Gossiper..117

56. Sometimes, Your Colleagues are the Real Face of Evil 119

57. Do Not Expect to Always Get Along with Your Supervisor 123
58. My Colleagues Perform the Same Job I Do and Make More than Me 125
59. Take the Time to Foster Positive Relationships Within Your Department and Companywide 127
60. Cultural Biases Can Hinder Your Growth 129
61. My Job is Secure 131
62. Laugh as Much as You Can in the Office, but Don't Make it a Party 133
63. Organizational Culture, Every Company is Unique 135
64. "Isms" in the Office 137
65. Never Work with Friends, Well Sometimes 139
66. Never Work with Your Spouse, Personal & Work-Life Will Become One 141
67. Never Work with Siblings, They Will Expect You to Do it All, While They Do Nothing 143
68. Office Relationships-Beware 145
69. Family-Owned Businesses are a Double-Edged Sword 147
70. My Boss is an Idiot 149
71. My Boss Thinks He/She Knows Everything 151
72. Don't be Condescending 153
73. Your Boss's Boss is an Excellent Person to Get to Know 155
74. If Your Supervisor Doesn't Like You, then Quit or Find Another Job ASAP! 157
75. Help! My Boss Takes Credit for My Work 159

76. Keep a Work Journal, It's More Important than You Think......161
77. Sexual Harassment..163
78. Always Leave with Dignity & Respect......................................165
79. You Will Know When It's Time to Leave.................................167
80. It's Only a Job...169

INTRODUCTION

Does your office make you feel like you are in some remote part of the world where you must always keep your wits about you because you do not know what perils await you? Or does it feel like high school all over again where there are cliques and bullying? This book will help you navigate through it all. Maybe your place of employment is not in an office setting. Perhaps you work construction, or you are a waitress. If you work with people, this book is for you. It is the human dynamic that drives this book and makes it colorful and informative. In this book, I list little tricks and anecdotes to make you laugh, but more importantly, to make you think. We spend a lot of time with people whom we cannot stand and have a strong dislike. Yet, our jobs can bring a great deal of wealth, knowledge, and benefits over time. I implore you to read these pages and allow yourself the opportunity to change your workspace dynamics.

For those of you who are reading this and don't, just know that you will. I have been unemployed. It is not a pleasant feeling. But do not worry, you will find a job. The key is to never stop looking. For the rest of you who do, this book is especially for you. This book can help improve your interpersonal relationships within an office environment. This book is formatted for you to read and then reflect. If you make this a quick read, you run the risk of missing something. If you simply read through this book and decide that none of the words written apply to you, you are fooling yourself. No one is perfect. We all have room for growth. We all have lessons to learn and lessons that we need to relearn.

This book will take you on a journey that will help you to understand that your actions and reactions to situations can have a positive or negative impact on others. By the end of the book, you should be able to identify the positive actions and reactions that you have towards others and situations, but also to identify the adverse effects and attitudes that you have towards others and how to rectify them. I will not use verbiage that will cushion the verbal blow of these words. On the contrary, my goal is blunt force honesty. Not everything will apply to you, but most things will. You do not have to be honest with me. You must be honest with yourself. When you are ready, read these pages and begin the process of creating a harmonious workplace, but more importantly, for yourself, having a more harmonious soul.

1. Do Your Job!

You receive a job description. (I know half of the tasks that you perform are not on your job description, including all the other work and tasks that you have. However, let's just pretend that it's a perfect world, and your job description lists all your duties.) We all have days where we are exhausted and completely stressed out. There may have been incidents that have made you hate your colleagues, boss, or the entire company. Even thinking about work can make you feel depressed and therefore make you want to perform lackluster on your job. Remember that rent and all the other bills are due. Do your job! Do your job to the best of your abilities. The integrity and quality of your work speak volumes, even if you think no one notices. Your colleagues are always watching you!

Along with doing your job comes understanding your position and role within your department. Have you been given new responsibilities to the point that you are not exactly sure what your role is anymore? If so, you must ask questions. What makes perfect sense to your boss often does not make sense to you. You are responsible for always being clear about your role and duties. Always be clear about your role, your tasks, and your responsibilities. It is easy to overlook it or to try to avoid having a conversation with your boss, especially when you do not necessarily like him. However, it is part of your job. It is an unwritten rule that you must always be clear about everything that pertains to you.

Samuel J. Varner

Are you in a situation where you must report to more than one person? If so, you need to iron out all the managerial issues. In cases like these, even managers are unclear; this is an opportunity for you to show your problem-solving and critical thinking skills. In situations like this, you might also have the chance to figure out the logistics on your own. If so, take full advantage of the situation. When no other solution is present, and you offer a great one, management is likely to along with it. It is a win-win situation for you. Do your best to make every situation work to your benefit. It is hard to see the silver lining in everything, but if you can train your mind to do so, you will be able to take advantage of opportunities that you did not even know existed.

Do you need training or education? If so, do not be ashamed to say so. Do whatever it takes to show that you are willing to go above and beyond. You cannot just say it. You must show it. Your word means nothing without actions to support them. Whether it is Microsoft Office Suite training or leadership training, you must be able to demonstrate how these training courses will help you to improve in your current role.

Suppose you have slacked off in your duties for any reason. It is time to pull yourself together and get your job done. It is hard when you have had bad experiences with your job. But until you find another one, do not give anyone a reason to get rid of you. People will look for anything to get rid of you and even lie on you. You should not give anyone ammunition to use against you.

Reflection: Do you simply do your job, or do you execute your job with a high level of critical thinking?

2. Come to Work on Time

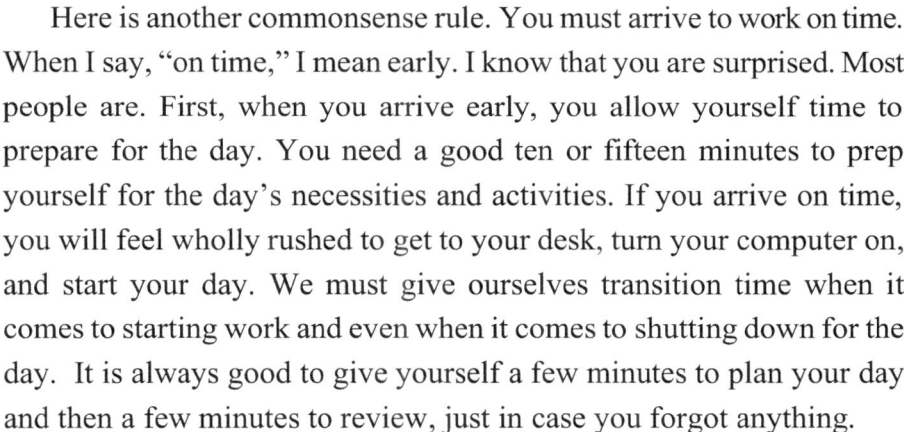

Here is another commonsense rule. You must arrive to work on time. When I say, "on time," I mean early. I know that you are surprised. Most people are. First, when you arrive early, you allow yourself time to prepare for the day. You need a good ten or fifteen minutes to prep yourself for the day's necessities and activities. If you arrive on time, you will feel wholly rushed to get to your desk, turn your computer on, and start your day. We must give ourselves transition time when it comes to starting work and even when it comes to shutting down for the day. It is always good to give yourself a few minutes to plan your day and then a few minutes to review, just in case you forgot anything.

You have noticed, or will notice, that someone is keeping track of your time and watching your every movement. But this is not about them; this is about you! Taking a few minutes in the morning to prepare for the day's activities will help you to alleviate stress. One of the reasons we feel stressed in our lives is because we never give ourselves time to transition from one event to the next. We consistently feel compelled to rush and complete as many tasks as possible in the shortest amount of time. We do not allow ourselves to transition from one task to another and to take small breaks in between. When you consistently move from one task to another, after a while, you will notice that your level of patience is almost nonexistent. You feel stressed, and after some time, you lose the ability to focus. A mind is a mighty machine, but it also needs time to process and even reboot.

We all run late. We need extra time because of anything that is happening in our lives. Some of you think that you can create your schedule. If you can, that's great! I wish I could. But for those of you who are habitually late, leave early, and take longer lunch breaks than allowed, you are only setting yourself up for trouble. I will repeat it; someone is watching you. We all have come into the office and said good morning and noticed that our colleagues would look at the clock before looking at us to say good morning, in return. That gets on my last nerve, but that is what people do. If someone who doesn't like you notices that you are late often, believe me, they will wait for the perfect opportunity to share this with your supervisor or anyone else, so that they can paint you in an unfavorable light.

We all have busy schedules, but if you want to remove some of the morning stress in your life, here is what you do. Prepare for work the night before. Your clothes should be ironed and set aside the night before. If you bring your lunch, then you need to have it prepared the night before. Place your keys, wallet, purse, and everything else that you need in one central location. If you have kids, teach them how to prepare the night before. This good habit will relieve a lot of stress in the mornings. I know you think this is impossible to do. It isn't. You simply must start with one good habit and keep adding new ones.

Do not have long conversations in the morning that will distract you from being on time. Do not try to do too many things before you come to work. Do what you can to plan your time, so that you can arrive on time. And by on time, I mean early. If you try to cram a few extra things, you will be late, and this could mean the difference between a promotion or not.

Reflection: What can I do to ensure that I arrive on time (early)?

3. Start on the Right Foot

Your first impression means everything, so make sure that it is the one you want others to have of you. They often stay with us, whether good, bad, or indifferent. Over time, your perceptions about others, and even you, may change.

I want to take a moment to talk about a type of impression that most people ignore. It is your lasting impression. You see, when someone first meets us, they have formulated their perception based on our outward appearance, as well their perception of themselves and others. If we remind someone of a person, someone that they used to know, then we take on that other person's impression. Over time, as people get to know us, those impressions fade away. The first impression is overwritten and replaced with a lasting impression. It is this impression that is just as important as the first impression.

Concerning first impressions, be polite, be respectful, but also be yourself. You always want to make a great first impression, but you must also take it one step further. You need to maintain it, so that it becomes a lasting impression. Your words and your actions must not contradict each other. It is something we cannot stand in others, but we must ensure that we do not exhibit the same behavior, as well. Your reputation is everything, and when your words and actions are aligned, people trust you, respect you, and are willing to work with you, especially when you are going through difficult times.

At first, you come to work on time, you do what you are supposed to do, and you do not take advantage of loopholes in company policy and procedure; but life happens, and things change. Your behavior changes, your work ethic can change, and the star employee that you once were may no longer exist. If you deviate from stellar performance, expect that others' perceptions of you will change.

Your reputation is in a fluid state, not a solid one. If you do begin to perform in a manner that is below the standard that you have displayed, people will not trust you. They will not want to work with you, and you will wonder why you are not receiving the promotions that you feel you deserve. You need to remain above reproach. What you started out doing, you must continue to do. When people see you change, they will change their actions towards you. Always remember that. It is not that the other person has changed; it's that you have shown that you are not the person you have displayed yourself to be.

Reflection: Am I consciously aware of the first impression that I express? Does my reputation speak for itself (in a positive light)? Are my words and actions aligned?

4. Never Be Afraid to Ask Questions!

No matter what your ego tells you, you do not know everything. Asking a question does not make you appear stupid. The contrary is true: It shows intelligence. Asking questions displays a willingness to learn. A desire to learn is also a willingness to grow. Knowledge is power, and you want all the knowledge that you can get. When it comes to your job, ask questions until you are clear about your role and responsibilities. If the person who previously performed your job is still employed with the company, make sure that you utilize them.

Do not feel that you have something to prove to the point that you alienate the one person that can help you to adapt quickly to your new position. If they are no longer with the company, ask if there is a desk reference, or to see any e-mails that can guide how to complete specific tasks. You want to put your best foot forward, and this is a great way to do it.

Reflection: Do you believe that asking questions makes you appear unintelligent? If so, why?

5. Maintain a Professional Tone at All Times, Regardless of the Medium

We interact with each other via e-mail, meetings, chat, video conferencing, etc. No matter the medium you use, you always want to communicate effectively. Your tone is foremost. You will hear people say that e-mail and other written forms of communication do not have a tone. That is a lie. We often can tell by the wording of an e-mail if there is a hostile tone or not. We know when our boss sends us an e-mail as a simple reminder and when it is not. Always maintain your composure. Anyone who can control your emotions has complete control over you and your actions.

This applies to your personal life, as well. A boyfriend, girlfriend, or anyone else who can make you angry controls you. They do this because they know that you are insecure about something in your life, and they use this insecurity to their advantage. In the office, the same applies. It is easy when we feel offended to fire back with an angry response. Sometimes, we can misinterpret the tone of any written communication. But often, we clearly understand the tone. It is easy to respond in kind with an equally hostile response. It can also cause you to say things that you cannot take back. Furthermore, it can place you in unfavorable light that will make others unfavorably think about you.

Samuel J. Varner

It is effortless to communicate with someone that you like. It is challenging to communicate with someone that you dislike. Here are some tips for verbal communication:

1. Be crystal clear about the message that you wish to convey. Your choice of words will have a direct impact on how a person will comprehend what you are attempting to convey.

2. Ensure that your body language is open and communicative. Uncross your arms and legs. Do not roll your eyes or make facial expressions that will make the other person feel that they are unworthy of your time.

3. Be sure to listen to all questions and answer appropriately. There is a difference between answering a question and responding to one.

4. Ensure that your tone is pleasant, warm, and inviting.

5. Respect that the other person, depending upon the topic, might not fully agree with you.

Remember, your goal is to win a person over, not to aggravate or agitate them. You want them on your side and not against you.

For written communication, you should do the following:

1. Always be clear and concise. Take a moment to think about what message you wish to convey in your correspondence. You want

to ensure that the recipient(s) clearly understand the message that you want to send.

2. Always make sure before you send an e-mail that you are sending it to the correct recipient(s). You do not want to send the wrong e-mail to the wrong person. Trust me, I have done this before.

3. Ensure that your tone is always professional and not hostile or adverse. Even if the e-mail that you are responding to possesses that same tone. It is essential to leave your emotions out of your professional communication with your colleagues.

4. Do not send a disparaging comment about anyone in the office via e-mail. It will be used against you.

5. Ask yourself, is this the best method to communicate your thoughts, ideas, or to disseminate information? Sometimes, e-mail may not be the best form of communication for what you desire to convey. A short conversation may be best. Over time, you will learn, which is the best form of communication, depending upon the message that needs to be conveyed.

6. Keep your e-mail as short as you possibly can without compromising your message. E-mails that are four pages long tend to turn people off and often get ignored.

Reflection: Are you conscious of the tone that you use when communicating with others? Do you communicate with others in the same tone that you want others to communicate with you?

6. Proofread Your Work

You have heard the saying, "The devil is in the details." This applies to your job. A little goes a long way. For example, when formatting a presentation, ensure that all the fonts are the same, that the format is consistent, and that you utilized the appropriate terminology. The little things convey that you are not just about the content of your work, but the appearance, as well. You will impress others and make your haters jealous. Sometimes, there is nothing more satisfying than having someone hate you just for you being you.

It does not matter if it is a proposal or a simple e-mail. Take a moment to review anything and everything that you are submitting for anyone to see. We all make errors and mistakes. However, some can be avoided simply by taking a moment to review your work, especially e-mails. We tend to send them without proofreading. E-mails that are well thought out and proofed are well received and show others that you care about your work and what you do. You can also use grammar checking software to polish your work. Sometimes, we do not make spelling errors, but you can make a grammatical error even of a suggestive nature by accident. Here are a few tips for proofreading your work:

1. Take a deep breath. Remember, you are creating a professional document that represents you. It does not matter if it is a letter,

an e-mail, or a PowerPoint presentation. This document is an extension of yourself and speaks to your professionalism.

2. Write an outline on a piece of paper or the *Sticky Notes* app, so that you can stay on track with the message that you wish to convey.

3. Try to block out others as much as possible. If you can avoid distractions, then do so.

4. Ensure that your tone is pleasant and professional.

5. Proofread it and ask someone to do the same. Your co-workers are an asset and not a liability.

6. Ensure that you listed all the recipients. Some people have the same name or similar names, so take a moment to ensure that you are sending the e-mail to the correct person.

Reflection: Do you take a moment and review your work? If not, why do you feel rushed to accomplish a task(s)?

7. Wash Your Hands... Literally!

I know that people will think of this rule as an odd one, but trust me, it is essential. It is imperative. Everyone has different standards concerning hygiene. You do not want to be known as a colleague who does not wash their hands. You do not want to be known as a colleague who has poor hygiene. You do not want a negative image. We have all seen the one person who will leave the stall and then go straight for the door. It is unhygienic.

Even if you go into the bathroom to check your appearance, you need to wash your hands. Others see this and will not want to work with you, deal with you, and at the annual potluck; no one will want to eat your food. People will let others know that you do not wash your hands. You want to have a good reputation, and something as simple as washing your hands can help to paint an overall great professional picture. In the workplace, unfortunately, it is more about looks and appearance than substance.

Even in this current environment, you need to make sure you wash your hands properly, not just using a dab of soap. A quick rubbing of the hands together and a rinse. You need to wet your hands and lather them with soap. Lather underneath your fingernails, and even between your fingers. Wash your hands (both sides) for at least 20 seconds.

Reflection: Am I washing my hands properly?

8. Your Appearance

Your appearance speaks volumes. I am just going to admit that there is a double-standard concerning what men can get away with and what woman can. I will admit there were days that my pants were clean, but not ironed. Sometimes, the sentiment of men is, "At least it's clean." These are the thoughts of most men. However, you must go beyond that. If you are on a path to excellence, then you must always exude excellence.

For men, iron your clothes before you leave the house and maintain your physical appearance. For men, khakis and a dress shirt are standard and perfectly acceptable. Make sure that as your pants are ironed, that your shirt is, as well. Make sure you groom yourself. Find a look that works for you.

Ladies always keep it classy. You are not going out with your friends, so as a rule of thumb, make sure your skirt is the appropriate length for the office. You want to make sure that your blouse fits because you do not want to make your chest the focal point of your outfit. One thing I have seen my sister and other women do is wear a blouse or a top, and then put on a blazer. A blazer can change your look from relaxed to professional. It is worth it to find clothing that fits you and speaks to your personality. You can still be professional and be yourself all at the same time.

Reflection: Am I giving my all to look my absolute best?

9. Don't Do Drugs on the Job

Not all employers demand drug tests, but if you pop pills, drink, smoke marijuana, or do anything that is considered illegal, do not do it at work. There was an instance at one of my previous jobs where someone left a small bag of marijuana in one of the lady's bathrooms. It did not take long for this to spread throughout the office. Luckily, they did not know whose drugs they were, and no action was taken. Just like there is a separation of church and state, so too is personal and work. If you know someone is abusing a substance at work, you should talk to the appropriate person about what you have seen.

If you need a substance just to make it through the day, you most likely have an addiction, but never be afraid to ask for help. There are those of you who are functioning addicts. This means that you have an addiction, but your lifestyle does not reflect it. We all have issues that are the catalyst for substance abuse. Therapy is essential, and there are programs out there that can help you. Employee assistance programs can help you. Get the help that you need. I am not judging anyone. Life is rough. Sometimes, we lean on drugs to make it day-to-day, but you need to be willing to deal with the issues that led you to your addiction. It is not easy. But there is help.

Reflection: What bad habits do I have that could harm my employment?

10. Your Reputation is the Most Significant Currency that You Have, Don't Become Devalued

What others think of you is important in the workplace. How you are perceived can lead to a promotion. How do you want others to perceive you? Think about this when you are in meetings and other work-related gatherings. Perceptions are more important than truth. People will believe what they see or what you convey. It is your responsibility to ensure that what you portray is positive and intelligent. You want others always to think the best of you and have great things to say about you. If they do not, trust me, you will go nowhere fast. If you do not think you have a reputation in the office, think again.

Everyone has a reputation. Your job is always to portray the best you. Never allow someone to make you lose your character. Never give in to your emotions, even if someone insults you. Always be the better person. Trust me, your colleagues will try to make you come out of character, but never do it. You can never really come back from a tarnished reputation. It can follow you, even after you have left the company.

Samuel J. Varner

If you have tarnished your reputation, all is not lost. It is not the end of the world. Just know that you will have to live with the stigma. You will need to take some time to reflect and grow. People will always remember what you have done and will not acknowledge who you have become. You will have to accept this. You will have to change your behavior, and if you need to apologize to anyone, do it. Depending upon the situation, silence can help you, as well; primarily, if you are always known for having something to say. It is not impossible to come back. Just know that it will take time. All things take time.

Reflection: Am I doing my best to ensure that I have and maintain an excellent reputation?

11. Give Credit Where Credit is Due

Do not steal your colleague's ideas and pass them off as your own. Especially if you are a manager or supervisor. Your subordinates look up to you and look to you for direction and guidance. You do not want to create an environment of distrust since you set the tone for your department. Karma will find you, and she will wait for the opportune time to give you back what you have given to someone else.

Sometimes, we feel inferior to others. First, we should not compare ourselves to others. It is like comparing apples to a car. We are all unique and different and possess different attributes, skills, and knowledge. Secondly, you have something valuable to contribute, and to think anything less is invalidating your existence and who you are. No one is smarter than another. We are all different, and our knowledge bases are different. You have something to contribute, so never think less of yourself. Give credit where credit is due. Allow your colleagues to shine and find a place where you can shine, as well.

It is natural to feel jealous and envious of others. It is a natural human emotion. You just do not have to act upon those feelings. It is easy to do so. But this is where you need to show restraint. If you find this hard to do, it is because you do not think enough of yourself. You do not love yourself enough. When you do, you will not allow the accomplishments of others to make you feel less than. You are also selfish because you are making something about you that has nothing to do with you.

Here is how to deal with these emotions. First, accept them. If you lie to yourself and do not admit it, you cannot confront these feelings and deal with them. Once you have acknowledged, then ask yourself why you are making this about you. Once you start being honest with yourself, it becomes easy to accept the accomplishments of others, while not seeing it as a personal attack against yourself.

Reflection: Why do I take credit for work that is not mine? Why is it hard for me to give credit where credit is due? What is it within me that makes me feel that there is no value in my work?

12. If You Don't Value Yourself, Why Should Anyone Else?

You must know who you are and your self-worth. You must know your strengths and weaknesses. You must be aware of who you are and be present in the knowledge that you are a person who is capable of great things. If you do not believe you are the best, you cannot and will not demonstrate it. You must value yourself, and that is something that you must learn to do.

You have had or will have experiences where your supervisor will criticize everything that you do when he/she makes you feel that you are inferior, and that you lack the necessary skills to perform your job. There will be many things that will happen throughout your professional career that will cause you to question every decision professionally that you have ever made.

It is when we experience adversity that we begin to think about what we truly value and want. No matter what happens, you cannot lose sight of who you are and your capabilities. A negative situation might be the opportunity for you to realize that maybe it is time to move on from the company.

It might be an opportunity to evaluate yourself professionally. It is essential to see every opportunity, even a negative one, as an opportunity for growth and advancement. You must see beyond the circumstances and see the road ahead.

Above all else, you must learn to hold yourself in the highest of esteem. No one else can and will do it for you. People will say good things about you, but you must say *great* things about yourself.

Reflection: How do you value yourself?

13. A Little Kindness Goes a Long Way

Sometimes, we are so engrossed with the e-mails we have to respond to, the systems we have to manage, the payments we have to approve, and the meetings we have to be in that we forget the most essential thing there is in the office, people. It is easy to forget our humanity and operate like machines. All we think about is producing and getting the job done, and we forget that the person sitting next to us is human, just like we are. We forget that our colleagues have struggles and life events, and can be depressed or lonely, just like us.

We forget that they have feelings just like we do. It does not matter if our skin color is different or our religious beliefs. We are all people, and we forget that a little kindness can make a huge difference in someone's day and even in their lives. We are all human, and we have bad days, and life events can make us mean and bitter. It does not mean that we aren't human.

Sometimes, we simply need someone to say or do something thoughtful for us to help us get through our day. Do not forget to do something kind for your colleagues. It can be something small and sweet. Trust me; people will remember the kind things that you do for them. You should not perform acts of kindness just to receive something in return. People will remember your kindness and seek to return the favor in kind.

There is no *Reflection* on this one. Stop, take a moment, and be kind to someone. I will take it one step further. Be kind to someone that you do not like.

14. Privacy... Don't Expect Any

At the office, it is easy to log into social media sites and update your status, read posts, and play games. But your employer is watching and trust me, when it comes time for your appraisal; this will come up. You are at work. You must stay focused on your job. Do not become sidetracked by social media. But it could also be the reason that you receive a low appraisal or worse, fired. Never post anything derogatory about your colleagues, supervisor, or the organization. They can find out about it, especially if you are friends with your colleagues on any of the social media sites.

If you are one of those people who assumes that there is such a thing as privacy in the workplace, let me take the time to tell you that it is not. At home, yes, you have privacy, but not at work. You do not own the desk that you sit at, nor the phone or the computer. Let me put it this way; you do not own anything. It all belongs to the organization. You have entered into a contract with your employer that states, if I perform ABC, then you will pay me XYZ. You allow me to utilize your equipment to perform said tasks. Now that we have this understanding, let me state this very clear.

You should not expect to have any form of privacy in any way, shape, or form! Your employer can, will, and does track all your communication. Companies can monitor the websites that you visit, and there is technology in the works that will allow employers to determine how productive you are. Besides that, everyone who comes to your desk will be curious about what you are doing. Do not expect privacy at work. It is an unrealistic expectation.

Be conscious of what you do at your job, period. My current employer allows you to surf the web during your lunch hour. Be informed about your organization's policies regarding the internet and even phone usage. At one of my previous employers, there was a colleague that they wished to terminate. They pulled her phone records and internet usage at the company for the past year. Luckily, she was not terminated, and they found no evidence that she misused her phone or internet privileges. I just want to reiterate that you are not at home on your personal computer or your phone. Everything at your job belongs to your employer, and those things are company property. They have every right to gather any information they desire concerning your usage. Again, do not expect privacy. Be cautious of your communication and overall think before you say or do anything that could have repercussions in the future.

Reflection: Do I use discretion in the workplace?

15. Use the Resources Around You

No matter what you might think, you do not know everything. There is always someone who knows something that you do not. So, always be on alert and always be willing to adapt. When it comes to your job, unless you are the most senior person there, there is someone who has been at the job longer than you, and this person can be a wealth of information. They can give you the history and background knowledge that others lack, and they can help you to understand the dynamics of your office. Offices, like high school, have cliques, and this person can help you to understand the relationships that people have and have had in the past.

Aside from that, history is essential, and gaining background knowledge can help you along the way. You can learn how specific policies and procedures came into play, as well as the mistakes others have made, so that you can avoid doing the same. If you want to succeed, you must use every resource at your disposal. Be creative and think as if no "box" exists. The truth is there is not a box, only the one that you have constructed. It is up to you to determine how you want to expand your knowledge base. Use every opportunity that your company offers to your advantage. If your company doesn't, then pursue it on your own. You are responsible for your growth and not the company. You only get out of life what you are willing to put into it.

Reflection: Do I take full advantage of the resources around me?

16. Use Office Supplies for Office Use Only

We have all taken a pen from work unintentionally. It happens. Of course, it is cost-effective to print things at work or use the postage machine. Companies are cracking down on personal use and making it part of the employee handbook. If you print one page, companies do not frown upon that, but when you print fliers, taking paper and other supplies from the company, that is stealing. You can be everything from reprimanded to terminated. Some companies give employees personal codes, so that they can track printing. It is best to buy your own printer and your own supplies. Do not forget that others are watching you, especially if you have enemies in the office. They will look for any excuse to report you. Do not give anyone any reason to say anything negative about you. Also, it is stealing, and who wants to be fired over supplies that you could afford to purchase?

Reflection: Have you stolen supplies from the office, and if so, how did you justify your actions?

17. If You Are an Introvert, You Can't Be At Work

Some people are naturally quiet individuals who stay to themselves and do not interact too much with others. Unfortunately, these people tend not to climb the corporate ladder. They tend to stay in the same position and have a lackluster career. If you do not come outside of your comfort zone, you can be overlooked for promotions. You must be social. People need to know who you are and have a good feel for you. They need to know something about you. If you stay to yourself, you will be perceived as weird, standoffish, and maybe someone who is not content with their job. None of the above may be true for you. Form bonds with your colleagues and even your supervisor. People must see the different dimensions that comprise your being. Here are a few tips to help you overcome your shyness. If you are awkward, that's okay. I'm a little awkward, too.

1) Learn how to feel comfortable in your skin. Accept yourself for who you are, quirks and all. It's easier said than done, but it is necessary if you want to make the most of your professional career.

2) Saying hello is often a good step. People like to talk about themselves, so ask them: How long have you been with the **company**?

What do you like most about the company? Where do you work? Or even a simple compliment is a significant first step.

3) Be present in the conversation and give the non-verbal cues that you are listening. A smile or a simple head nod is sometimes all it takes.

4) Contribute to the conversation. Share your experiences. You might not be the most exciting person in the world, but there must be something worth sharing. Understand that you have a voice, as well. Extroverts love to talk about themselves and everything that they know, and it is hard to get a word in. But you must sometimes wait for the pause in conversation and jump right in, and sometimes, you must create the pause.

5) Have a few extrovert friends at work. Introverts are not naturally social and do not showcase their talents, skills, and expertise. But your extrovert friends will; they will be your most prominent advocate and your mouthpiece. They will tell others about your talents and skills. So, allow them and even ask for their help. Extroverts like to talk anyway, so give them something to talk about and promote yourself in the process.

These few little tips will go a long way in helping you to stand out. Don't forget, even if you are not a confident person, pretend that you are. If you do not feel confident, pretend that you are until you believe it. Stand up straight, smile, and feel comfortable in your skin. If you do not portray it, it is not real to anyone around you.

Reflection: Do I make attempts to be social with my colleagues?

18. Learn Another Language

If you genuinely want to test yourself, then learn another language. This is one of the most challenging things to do as an adult. As Americans, we speak our language, but are very much unfamiliar with the syntax that is associated with it. Suppose someone asked you what a participial phrase, gerund, or an indirect object is. You might assume that you are being asked a scientific question and not an English language question. You might be able to guess one of them correctly, even though you use all of them daily. We often do not know the technical aspects of the language that we speak.

The world is becoming more and more of a bilingual place. People in other parts of the world know many different languages, yet most American's only speak one language. Learning another language will help you to appreciate another culture, as well as your own. It will also look good on your résumé. Anything that you can do to make yourself look better on paper you should.

Here are a few tips when learning another language.

1. Make it fun for yourself.
2. Find a language partner.
3. Take a class (especially if your company will pay for it!)

Reflection: Am I doing all I can to maximize desirability within the marketplace?

19. You Only Get What You Put In

If you only put in 10%, you will only gain 10%. We want to put in 10%, but expect to receive 100%. That is not how life works, and this mentality will get you nowhere in life. You must be willing to give 100%, and then you will receive 100%. That is how life works; you only get what you put into it. If you want to succeed, you must give 100%. Think about those things in your life that you genuinely love, and without question, you give 100%. The reason it is easy to give 100% to something that you love is that you are passionate about it. You need to become passionate about your job. It is the only way that you are going to succeed. This is where you will learn the difference between performing job duties and excelling in your position.

I completely understand that you can have a job that you dislike. You could have been laid-off and needed another job, or there could have been lay-offs, and you got stuck with more work. Or you could be that person who has been in the same position for years, and you do not see the light at the end of the tunnel. If you want to survive the day, you must add passion to it. There is no way around it.

Reflection: Why do I expect to get the most, but I am only willing to invest the least? Why am I ok with not giving my all? What am I truly passionate about?

20. I Don't Receive the Praise I Should

There might be some relevance to this statement. Sometimes, people do not receive the recognition that they deserve. However, I want to mention those who do the minimum and expect the highest praise. You know someone like this, and you could be this person. You are expected to arrive on time, take the appropriate time for breaks and lunch. Perform your duties and other tasks as assigned. That is the standard.

Going above and beyond can mean volunteering for special projects, training new staff, staying late to help finish a project, etc. My point is stop trying to receive credit for the things that you are supposed to do. No one wants to hear it, and everyone you tell is thinking that you do less than what you do. Stop it already.

Another point I want to make is simply this; you will not always receive the recognition that you deserve. You must be confident within yourself and know that you have done an excellent job. If none of your hard work, dedication, accomplishments, or achievements are noticed, then this is a sign that you might want to seek employment elsewhere. You should always receive some form of recognition for all that you do.

Also, if you do not receive the praise you believe that you should receive, praise yourself. Be proud of your accomplishments. Be proud of the work that you do. When you do, you will realize that it does not matter if someone else recognizes your hard work or not, because you have already validated yourself.

Reflection: Do you feel valued by your current employer?

21. Education, Education, Education

Today, you need education. You will need a degree. There was a time when all you needed was a high school diploma. Nowadays, you need a bachelor's, and it seems like in the near and present future, you will need a master's degree for an entry-level job. Don't sell yourself short. Go to school, or go back to school, and finish your education. Companies will sometimes offer tuition reimbursement. Take advantage of it. Companies will also occasionally provide training and certification programs. Your duty as an employee is to take advantage of every opportunity afforded to you. All the education that you receive will help you along with your professional career. You must take advantage of every opportunity that you can. Mentorship is another way of receiving an education. The whole point of learning is growth. The more you know, the more you grow. The more you grow, hopefully, the more fulfilled you will feel, and with any luck, it will lead you along the career path that you desire.

Reflection: Am I taking full advantage of all the opportunities that I have at my fingertips?

22. Time

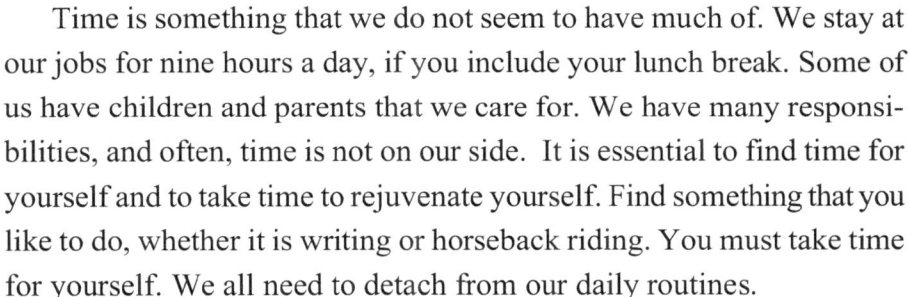

Time is something that we do not seem to have much of. We stay at our jobs for nine hours a day, if you include your lunch break. Some of us have children and parents that we care for. We have many responsibilities, and often, time is not on our side. It is essential to find time for yourself and to take time to rejuvenate yourself. Find something that you like to do, whether it is writing or horseback riding. You must take time for yourself. We all need to detach from our daily routines.

A short break throughout the workday is essential to managing a stressful workday or even a hectic one. When we are motivated and working on a project, it is easy to say that we do not have time for a break. Breaks help to rejuvenate us and to help us gain perspective on the work we are doing, as well as help to lower stress. Continuing to focus on a task without taking a break can lead to frustration, which is not conducive to your state of mind. Also, it prevents you from gaining a clear perspective on your work. Take a break; you've earned it. You deserve it, and it is necessary for maintaining your sanity.

Concerning the job, time is precious. Do not waste time at work. Make sure you understand your duties, especially if they constantly change. Do not wait until the last minute, either. Procrastination only adds to your level of stress. But do take the time to plan what you will do. Do not rush your work, take your time, but do not take too much time.

Reflection: Do you manage your time wisely, or do you let the day manage you?

23. Make Yourself Invaluable, But Within Reason

You want to be known for good work. You want to receive promotions. You want to be considered for special projects, and you want to advance. Being available to help is excellent, and it gives you great exposure, but you must be careful; otherwise, you will find yourself devoted to your job 24/7. A work-life balance is essential, and without it, you will experience burn out. Burn out is inevitable and happens to everyone along their career path. It can happen more than once.

You want to do enough to be seen, but not too much that you do not have a healthy life. It is a job, and working is essential. We all must work, but the point is other things matter more. If you do not give time to those things that matter most to you, you will live an unfulfilled life.

Here is how you show your willingness to grow without compromising your personal life.

1. Only volunteer for those tasks that you are passionate about.
2. Volunteer for projects that already correspond to your job or for projects that will allow you to move into a different field.
3. Accept that there are only eight hours in a day. Do not push yourself to complete and do everything in one day.

Reflection: Do you have a work-life balance? If not, why?

24. Burnout is Inevitable, But There are Ways to Manage It

I want to share my experience in dealing with burnout because sometimes, it can happen, and you are not even aware of it. I started a new job. It was a fresh start, and it was everything I needed. It was less stressful. I felt I could concentrate on my work. I was happy, and then things happened. My boss began to mention errors that I made, and then we instituted a new system that I had to train others. Changes were made to processes that directly affected my job. Then, I gained other duties. The quiet, calm, peaceful position slowly turned into a nightmare. I lost sleep, and I could not focus.

I had a co-worker who worked with me, and if it weren't for her, I would have been lost. I was so busy doing things that I was not conscious of doing. Entire conversations were lost, and I was angry, completely stressed, and unhappy. I was dreading coming to work, and I did not look forward to interacting with anyone. I slowly began to realize that I was to blame and not the company. I know some people will find that statement hard to believe, but it is true. I put my job before my spiritual, emotional, and physical health. I told myself that the role was more important than I was. I lost my focus. I know how to do my job, and I am great at my job, but I had to learn to be great at the role of putting me first.

I had to change my way of thinking and began to manage me. When I did so, the work did not go away, but how I perceived it did. I had to regain my focus and align myself in such a fashion that I set myself up to succeed and to have balance. It is easy to lose focus and to become short-sighted. You can get another job. Your health and mental well-being are a one-time deal.

Your job is a priority. There is nothing wrong with your desire to want to do your best. Sometimes, you might have to stay late, and maybe you might have to work on a weekend here and there. But if you allow your job to be your entire life, you will burn out completely. I know some of you are reading this book have, or are currently experiencing burn-out. Here are some tips to help you balance work life and personal life to become realigned.

1. Spend time with friends. Those friends that you have taken for granted, it is time to call them and say let's hang out. Buy them drinks; you owe it to them and yourself.

2. Work your regular hours. I know that this one might be hard for some of you workaholics out there and that promotion might be in reach, but if you don't find a way to have a work-life balance, you might just one day walk away from the job or have a heart attack or stroke.

3. Meditation and prayer–Before you start your day, take ten minutes, and just breathe. Try not to think of anything. You have forgotten who you are as a person. It is time to remember who you are.

4. You need a hobby. You need to focus on your personal life. What do you like to do for fun? It doesn't matter what it is. You just need to do it and leave the office at the office.

5. Take time off and take a vacation. The fact that you are burnt-out means you have plenty of annual leave. It is time to start using it. If you have no place that you want to go, then take a staycation. One of my favorites is to come in two hours later and leave two hours early. A couple of half-days can help you. You need time to unwind and de-stress. It does not matter how you do it; just do it. You owe it to yourself.

Reflection: Are you burnt-out? Do you have a work-life balance?

25. NEVER Accept a Friend Request From a Supervisor & Most Colleagues

It is difficult currently to not be "friends" with your colleagues on social media sites. It is how we communicate and share thoughts and ideas. You must be careful about what you post. One wrong post about the company or another colleague can land you in trouble. Just because you delete the post does not mean it disappears. It never does. Your frenemy at your job could be looking for that one thing that they can use against you. I have seen people print posts and use them against their colleagues. Be careful of what you say and what you post. It is your page, and you can do what you want and say what you want, but remember others are watching and could use this against you.

Reflection: Are you conscious about what you post and who you connect with via social media?

26. Faith... We All Need It

Faith is important. I am not talking about faith in God. I'm talking about having faith in yourself. It is easier to have faith in God than to have faith in yourself. If you belong to a religious organization, then you learn about God and religion and about having faith and all that pertains to it. But you will never learn in school how to believe and have faith in yourself. There are no classes for self-awareness and self-actualization in the education system. It is a class that is not taught, and it is assumed that one day in life, you will just do it naturally.

You learn to have faith and love yourself with time and experience. If you do not believe that you are successful, smart, intelligent, and attractive, then why should anyone else? You should believe the absolute best about yourself and leave the negativity to the haters around you. Let them think what they want to think about you. Only you can determine what is true about yourself. What you believe about yourself is what you manifest.

Reflection: What situation or circumstance has caused me to not believe in myself?

27. Leave the Office at the Office

You will say that this is impossible. Depending on your job, it might be. Some of us work around the clock and have insane schedules. Your perspective isn't fresh, and no matter how much coffee you drink, it cannot give you the same results as a good night's sleep or a day off. Work-life balance is essential for being alert and, more importantly, maintaining good health.

As we get older, we must take better care of ourselves, and finding a balance is one of them. Also, we have personal lives. If you have a passion or a hobby, pursue it. It will allow you time to detox from your job and give you that fresh perspective that you need. If you work all the time, you will be a dull person, and no one wants to be with anyone who works all the time. If you must admit anything to yourself, we all want to find that special someone whom we can share our lives. You cannot do that if you are working all the time. But it is a great way to become a hermit and a humbug if you want. I just wanted to use the word humbug. It is an interesting word: at least to me.

Reflection: Who are you outside of the office, or are you your job?

28. Volunteer for Special Projects

I have mentioned it before, but I will repeat it—volunteer for special projects. I know you are thinking, I already have too much work to do as it is. I don't disagree with you; however, this is another opportunity for you to network in the office. You can have contact with people you would not ordinarily interact with. This is also a platform to showcase your talent, skills, and willingness to grow. It also allows people to see you in a different light and helps you to stand out from the crowd. It can also be the steppingstone you need to move up within the organization. Being a good worker is not enough. You must show that you are willing to step outside of the box of where you are. Show others that you can be and are more than just your current role.

If you are a shy person, here is my advice to you. You cannot afford to be bashful, and it will only hinder you. Shyness does not serve you in the workplace and life in general. We all are shy on some level, and that is natural. Being shy prevents you from showcasing who you are. If someone does not know you, you are invisible to them. If you are invisible to others, they do not see you, and they do not know your capabilities. Never be afraid to let your natural talent shine.

Reflection: What interests do you possess outside of your current role? Are there opportunities to change career paths? Are you ready to demonstrate to your colleagues that you are more than your current role in the organization?

29. Know Your Limit & Use Discretion

Most companies have at least one or more social gatherings for employees. While these are not mandatory, they are imperative for you to meet new people and to make a name for yourself. It is the perfect time to network within the organization. It is not a happy hour, and you are not out with your friends. You must remain professional. You must know your limit if you drink alcohol. You cannot allow yourself to become intoxicated at these types of gatherings. It will only hurt your career in the long run. People are still watching you and trust me; someone is adding up how much alcohol you have consumed. We have all heard the office story that someone regrets.

With technology, your little fiasco can be recorded, or someone can go "live" and share this with the entire world. So, drink sparingly or do not drink at all. Do not drink before you attend the event, either. You should not arrive drunk; that is just as bad. If you need a drink, go out with your friends afterwards where you can drink as much as you want, and no one will judge you. Well, one friend. We all have that one judgmental friend.

Reflection: Am I conscious of my drinking habits at professional gatherings?

30. Clean Your Desk Regularly: An Unscheduled Absence Might Not Work in Your Favor

I worked in an office where one manager disliked another. Every time said the manager was out of the office, she would look on his desk, hoping to find something. Every time she discovered anything, she could use against him, she would run into our senior manager's office. The senior manager in our department was very relaxed. He did not like to entertain her. He only wanted to ensure that the work was completed.

I shared this story because there are people who will not like you for any reason. With that in mind, you must protect yourself. Because someone is always looking to take you down, do not leave your desk messy. Always leave it clean and tidy at the end of the day. Do not leave paperwork lying around, put it away, or lock it up regardless of your job. Also, being neat and tidy adds to your professional image.

Reflection: What message does your workspace convey about you?

31. Always Remain Calm

Situations will arise in the workplace. It is inevitable. Any place where people congregate for any length of time, there will be disagreements and misunderstandings. It is part of life, and you must simply accept it. Sometimes, a person will dislike you because you are a woman, black, gay, attractive, or intelligent. You might have offended them, intentionally or unintentionally. You might have lied to a colleague. There are a plethora of reasons that can lead to an issue or misunderstanding. Here is my point. It is not an opportunity for you to show your colorful side. It is neither the time nor the place for you to lose control. If you do anything that betrays the character that you have shown thus far in the workplace, you are setting yourself up for failure. People will think this is the real you and the persona that you have been professing is fake and phony. You always want to remain calm. If someone can make you angry, they can control your actions. They can make you out to be the villain when that is not the case. Always remain calm.

Of course, it is easier said than done, but here are a few tips:

1. Take several deep breaths. You do not have to show up to every fight, argument, or disagreement.

2. Walk away. You can take away someone's power with this simple action.

3. If it is an e-mail, do not be quick to respond. We are a generation of keyboard thugs and will not hesitate to respond to anything we believe is disrespectful. There will be times when no response is the best response. (Here is a tip I have learned, and I use it continually in life. Silence is power! By offering someone who has an issue with you silence, it infuriates them. The act of doing nothing is sometimes the most powerful action that we can take in our professional and personal life.

4. Ask yourself if silence is an appropriate response. There are many other things that you can do. Take the time to discover what helps you to calm down and then do it. I made a stress ball entirely out of rubber bands. It helps me to relieve stress.

Reflection: How do you manage stressful situations? How do you make a stressful situation work in your favor?

32. Mentorship is Essential

Mentorship is a must for professional growth. You can find a mentor who is in a profession that you wish to enter, or you can find a mentor whom you believe will aid you in your professional growth. Professional growth is essential, and we all can learn something from someone. If your company offers a mentorship program, then take full advantage of it. If not, then create your own opportunity. A simple conversation can yield amazing results. You never know when lunch once a month or every couple of weeks with an executive can help you gain knowledge and insight about yourself. Remember, you want to make connections, and you want to grow professionally to be your absolute best. You cannot do that if you are waiting for an opportunity. Sometimes, you just have to make one. When an opportunity presents itself, be open to it.

A mentor can offer you guidance about career advancement and growth. I will be honest with you. People frequently like to talk about themselves and the things that they have experienced. It is an opportunity to listen and absorb the life experience of another, and then apply it to your life. You never know what one conversation can do for the rest of your professional career.

But before you take on a mentor, be clear about what you want to achieve from the mentorship. They are going to want to know why you chose them and what you hope to gain, as well as your goals. You must be clear with yourself about all those things. It is the time to be introspective and to be honest with yourself about what you genuinely want and desire. It takes time and energy, but it is time well spent when you consider how many hours you will be working until retirement.

If you are pursuing your own mentorship program, take a moment to let your supervisor know. Now, be prepared for jealousy and some type of backlash depending upon your boss's personality. Some will have no problem with you wanting to gain professional experience, while others will see you as being disloyal and wanting to move to another department. The latter may very well be the case.

Reflection: Are you taking advantage of the mentorship program offered by your employer? If one doesn't exist, seek out a mentor or better yet, create a mentorship program at your job.

33. Networking

I have mentioned networking, and I want to clearly define what networking is and why it is beneficial for you to form your professional network. Networking, in a nutshell, is the ability to create a professional connection with someone. You must network within your organization and outside of it. You must allow people to get to know you on a professional level. It can help you to move up within your organization. Both are necessary if you want to establish yourself within an organization.

It is important to network outside of your organization. It is essential to meet and form connections with other professionals. You never know when a new opportunity might present itself, and you want your professional network to keep you in mind.

Networking is an invaluable tool whether you want to move up in an organization or want to find another job. Networking is a great way to get to know others who have the same goals as yourself, or who are in the career that you desire. It is important to know others. People can open doors for you that would not usually be open. So, be sociable and be willing to meet others. Your next opportunity could be waiting for you.

Reflection: Are you taking advantage of all the networking opportunities that are within your reach? Have you joined an organization that pertains to your career path?

34. If You Don't Ask For It, Don't Expect It

You only get what you ask for. If you do not ask for a raise or a promotion, do not expect to receive one. Your supervisor cannot read your mind and does not know what your true desires are. You must learn to open your mouth and ask for what you want. If you don't ask for it, don't expect to receive it. I will repeat it. If you don't ask for it, don't expect to receive it.

When you ask for a raise or a promotion, be ready to state everything that demonstrates why you deserve a promotion. Have your list ready. You want to "toot your own horn". You can even include praise that you have received from co-workers and managers. Think of this meeting as a debate. You need to clearly state your case and have quality and reliable information to back it up. Do not go in with a negative or defeated attitude. If you do, you have set yourself up for failure, or rather you have set yourself up to receive nothing, because you do not believe that you will receive anything.

You must go in with a winning attitude. Now, you might not get the raise that you want or the promotion, but do not let yourself walk away empty-handed. There must be something that the company can do for you. Do not be quick to take "no" for an answer. Ensure that you do not go in with an entitled attitude. You want something, and the last thing you want to do is to aggravate the one person who can provide you with what you desire.

If you are nervous and you find it difficult to state your case, then practice with a friend or a co-worker whom you extremely trust. Practice what you are going to say and make an outline of all your accomplishments. Remember, you do not want to go in nervous; you want to go in confident, but not arrogant.

Never be afraid to state what you know you deserve. You are your greatest advocate, and you never know; that raise or promotion you want could simply be in reach, but you missed the opportunity, because you did not proclaim your great work.

Reflection: Have you suffered in silence by not articulating your desire for a raise or a promotion? Why do you find it difficult to "toot your own horn"?

35. Don't Steal Your Colleague's Lunch

We all have heard the stories of one of our colleague's lunch that has gone missing. If this is you, stop it. People will find a way to retaliate. They are not above putting laxatives in the food or other things to find the culprit and make him pay. Times are tough, but taking that which does not belong to you is wrong, and when your colleagues find out it is you, prepare for a whirlwind of hatred and vengeance. You will deserve it because you created the situation.

It boils down to respect. What is yours is yours, and what belongs to another, belongs to another. Don't be a "do so, don't like so," which means if someone stole your lunch, you would be up in arms, but it's okay for you to "do so" to others. It is not right. Treat others with respect, regardless of how they treat you.

Reflection: How respectful am I truly to my colleagues?

36. Revenge is a Dish Best Served Cold, But Sometimes, It's a Dish That Doesn't Need to Be Served at All

No matter the place of employment, no matter how isolated your work might be, as long as you must interact with others, there will always be conflict. Sometimes, your colleagues will lie on you. Sometimes, they will seek to take credit for your work. Sometimes, they will do whatever they deem necessary to make themselves look better than yourself.

Your natural and very human instinct is to seek revenge. Don't do it! I know revenge is fun, and it can feel satisfying, but it will also take you to a place that is difficult to come back. Do your job and focus on your work; otherwise, revenge will be your focus. Your work will suffer, but more importantly, you will suffer. When you seek revenge, you are saying to yourself that, at this present moment, this person or situation is more important than me. I must give them all of my time and energy and make them the focus of my existence. You are the most important person, period! So, don't waste your time and energy on someone who is not deserving of it. People will say and do whatever is necessary for their benefit. You must accept that.

Furthermore, you must understand that others are insecure. When someone acts out of their insecurities, we tend to take it personally. From their warped mindset, they perceive your actions as an attack on them. You are merely showcasing your natural talents and skills. There is nothing that you can do about this. But what you can do is not collude with this madness and invoke negative energy. Remember, it takes two to argue. Don't join in. Rise above it.

Reflection: Why am I so emotionally invested in my place of employment?

37. Respect the Religious Beliefs of Others

Everyone has their own set of beliefs or some choose not to believe in anything at all. So, whether you are Christian, atheist, or anything in between, respect that there are people who are different than yourself. Here is why. No one is going to say that my religious beliefs suck, and yours are better. We all assume the reverse, what I believe is right, and everyone who doesn't believe like me is confused and needs to be saved, converted, or whatever. We must all accept that people have different religious beliefs than our own. We can and often make comments and spew religious rhetoric that is counterproductive to forming positive working relationships.

It is easy to offend others without realizing it. Here is a rule of thumb. Do not discount, discredit, or disrespect your colleagues' religious beliefs. Accept that people have the right to believe what they want or to believe nothing at all. Keep your spiritual truths to yourself, and do not impose them upon anyone. You are at work to work, not to convert others to your belief system. Respect differences and accept others for who and what they are and believe, even if they believe nothing at all.

Reflection: Do I treat others with the dignity and respect that I desire from others?

38. Never Fear Success, Embrace It

We fear success and see failure as part of life. You won't win every game, ace every exam, or achieve every goal you have set for yourself. You won't get everything you want in life. We have learned to accept that as an absolute. We expect and accept it as being a part of life. When it comes to success, it is not something that we accept but see, instead, as a game of luck. We see success like winning the lottery or happening to be at the right place at the right time.

We do not see success as part of our lives. We see celebrities, and we know that they have worked hard for their success, but we also, more importantly, believe that it is just a game of luck, not something that is tangible and achievable like a failure. We believe that failure is always around us. When we step out to do anything, we always brace ourselves for failure. We prep ourselves; we try not to get our hopes up.

We have come to believe that which we desire most is out of our reach and most likely unattainable. Everything that we genuinely want is not for us. So when the impossible happens, we are shocked, we are overwhelmed. Because we do not believe in success, we do not think it can happen for us.

Samuel J. Varner

If you believe that success is out of your reach, it will always appear to be. You are what you believe. If you do not believe in yourself, why should anyone else? If you are constantly second-guessing yourself, you are setting yourself up for failure. You will not succeed if you do not get out there and do what you know you can do. Will you fail? It depends on how you view failure.

My definition of the word *failure* is when you do nothing. If you try and give it all that you've got, you have not failed, but tested yourself. You have created an experience by which you can garner knowledge. You can succeed. Trust yourself; don't let others stop you from being who you are. But more importantly, don't stand in your way of success.

Reflection: What steps can you take to stop standing in the way of your success?

39. If You Can, Get Others to Do Some, Whole, or Part of Your Work for You, Then Do So

This rule might seem underhanded and a little unscrupulous, but sometimes, when you have deadlines to meet, you will need help. It is okay to ask for help, even when you might not need it. Here's why. You want to be known as the person who either meets or completes their work before the deadline. Projects can change midstream, be canceled, or accelerated. The faster you can complete a project, or at least set a foundation for moving forward, the quicker you will be able to complete the task, or will have time to adjust to meet the different demands. It is important not to use others, but asking for help and sometimes getting help from others is necessary for your success. Do not forget to help others when you can. It is always polite to return a favor.

Also, you do not want to reinvent the wheel. The information you need could be within your grasp. I know that we all want to say we were the originator of something, but there is nothing wrong with taking something that was already started and turning into something relevant today.

Let's be honest for a second. We are not good at everything. We should not lie nor pretend that we are. It is your job to know your colleague's strengths, so that you will know how to utilize them. Notice,

I used the word *utilize* and not *take advantage of*. Do not take advantage of your co-workers. You are all on the same team regardless if you work in different departments.

Once you understand their strengths, it will be easier to gain their assistance with various tasks if they like you. Some are excellent at organizing and creating presentations. If so, ask for a template for you. It will save you hours of trying to figure out how to construct one. Do you have a co-worker who is an excellent writer? If so, ask him or her to proofread your work or an important e-mail. Do you have a co-worker who possesses a vast knowledge base? If so, then you need to make time to sit with him or her and gain as much knowledge as you can. As I stated before, but I want to take a moment to reiterate, do not forget to help them, as well.

Reflection: What are the strengths of your colleagues who work closest to you? What are your strengths? Why was it easier for you to identify the strengths in others, but not yourself?

40. If You Tell Anyone in the Office Your Business, You Might as Well Have Told the Entire Office

The office is a network of social bonds. People have known each other for years, may have attended college together, or have worked at other organizations together. It is essential to identify those connections, so that you can be mindful and to whom you say it. You should not tell anyone all your business. There are things that you should just keep private. Some people are an open book, and that is fine. You must always think before you speak. You must ask yourself, "Is this something I want the entire office to know?" If you tell one person, you have told everyone.

It is important to have boundaries in the workplace, and it is okay not to talk about personal things in your life. It's okay if you are a private person. I think more people should be a little bit more private. There will be times when you open up to others and share things on a personal level. That's fine, and it's natural. You should always think before you speak, but in the office, especially.

Reflection: How often do I practice discretion?

41. Don't Let Bad Situations Poison Your Soul

When you first start your new job, you are energetic, joyful, happy, and helpful. You are willing to go above and beyond. Because this is a new opportunity, this is a new environment. Everything is new, and it might even be a new career path that you have been dreaming about for years. When you go into this new job, you are excited and have the joy of a kid going to Disneyland. That's great; it is how we all are when we start a new job. But then life happens. You can have anything from a disagreement with a colleague to have your work questioned. Suddenly, you have new duties and responsibilities. You have colleagues who do not present you in the best light and use whatever they can against you.

Many things can and will happen that will make you think, "What am I doing here?" These situations and others can make you lose who you are and make you act out of character. If you feel attacked continuously, your natural reaction is to strike back by being defensive, verbally aggressive, standoffish, rude, and insensitive. You cannot let the actions of others dictate your own. You must remain focused on who you are. There is a clear line between being concise and being rude. Because others have hurt you, it does not mean that you have the license to do the same to others. Now, is an excellent time to examine yourself and to ask, "How do I treat others on my job? Do I treat them the way I want to be treated, or do I mistreat them the same way I have been mistreated?"

Dealing with people is not easy, especially when they don't like you, whether you gave them a good reason to or not. You must understand them and accept them for who they are. You must discover a way to interact with this person, so that you always shine. You cannot let someone else's negativity become your own. Because when you do, they become your "god".

Reflection: How do I treat others on my job? Do I treat them the way I want to be treated, or do I mistreat them the same way I have been mistreated?

42. Every So Often, Dress Like You Are Going on An Interview

It's a fun rule. I personally like this one, and I do it often. It's kind of fun. You dress as if you are going for an interview. It works if you work in a casual business environment. You want to know what kind of reaction you will receive. If your boss does not care, they will not be phased by it. They will simply say, "Oh, you look nice today," and then keep going.

But if your employer values you, then they will ask you how things are going and try to see what is going on professionally. It is an excellent opportunity for you to express any issues you may have or other problems. Make the most of this opportunity if it presents itself. If it does not, then maybe it is time to start looking for a new job, for real.

Reflection: Even in this current environment, you should still dress to impress from time to time; otherwise, you will get into a psychological rut. So get up, get dressed, wash your face, and brush your teeth every day. This will give you the sense of normalcy that you need.

43. Ethical Behavior

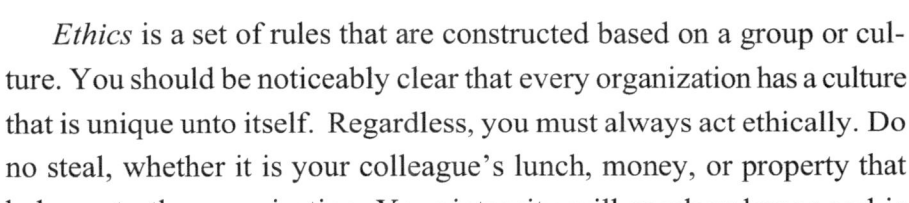

Ethics is a set of rules that are constructed based on a group or culture. You should be noticeably clear that every organization has a culture that is unique unto itself. Regardless, you must always act ethically. Do no steal, whether it is your colleague's lunch, money, or property that belongs to the organization. Your integrity will speak volumes and is part of being a professional. You must carry yourself above reproach.

Another aspect of ethics is *accountability*. Everyone wants accolades for a job well done, but when a mistake or an error happens, few will take responsibility. Often, the blame game comes into play. I urge you if you are the one who likes to blame others for your mistakes, you shouldn't. Maybe today and tomorrow you will get away with it, but it is only a matter of time before you will be held accountable. Take responsibility for your actions, even your mistakes.

Teamwork and the ability to interact well with others is another aspect that goes unnoticed. You must be able to work with others and to communicate effectively. You are not an island to yourself. It is not a one-person show. You must be clear, but more importantly, you must be respectful. Think of the recipient every time you send an e-mail. Treat every e-mail as if you are sending correspondence to the president of the company. I know the tone, attitude, sarcasm, and disrespect will quickly vanish from your communication.

Samuel J. Varner

There will be times when you will see or know that others are acting in an unethical manner. It is best to report it. I know that it is not easy to communicate what you see. I know that there can be backlash and retaliation from your actions. Sometimes, you can be punished for doing the right thing and saying something when everyone wants you to keep your mouth shut. Just remember that silence is acceptance.

Reflection: Do you act ethically? Are your actions above reproach?

44. Money Isn't Everything

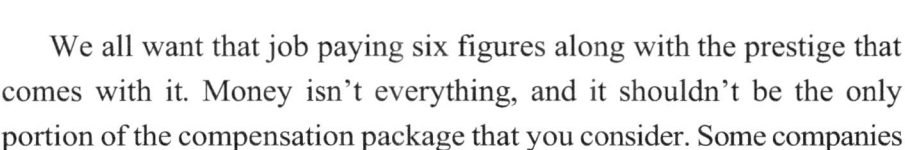

We all want that job paying six figures along with the prestige that comes with it. Money isn't everything, and it shouldn't be the only portion of the compensation package that you consider. Some companies offer perks that others do not. Do not be ashamed to ask along the interview process what is the company's compensation package.

Some jobs provide 401k matching, cover the full cost of health benefits, allow flexible work schedules, and even provide on-site daycare. One of my previous employers sponsored a health and wellness week in which we received free health screenings. They also offered massages for those who wanted them.

My point is that we all need money to survive, but the benefits that some employers provide are just as vital to allowing us to live a comfortable life. Consider all that a company has to offer. Those benefits are another form of compensation.

Reflection: Are you aware of your company's compensation package? Have you fully utilized all the benefits?

45. Sometimes, I Feel Like I am Still in High School

Some of us never grow up, and if we were the jock, the cheerleader, the class clown, or the bully, we tend to take that with us into adulthood. Bullying is a hot topic right now, but it does not just happen in high school. It occurs in the workplace. Anytime anyone does anything to make you feel less than or to strip you of your dignity, it is bullying.

Some of you that are reading this are being bullied on your job. The only way to stop a bully is to stand up to them. You must learn to be your biggest advocate. It's not easy; it's scary, especially when the person bullying you is your supervisor. There are always ways to deal with the situation. There is no one right way to handle this.

But remember, always be professional. You might have to talk to someone in Human Resources, or you may have to speak to your boss's boss.

Reflection: Am I, or have I ever been, a bully to anyone?

46. It's Review Time, Put Your Game Face On

Every year and sometimes quarterly, employees should receive an appraisal. As an employee, we look at this time as our supervisor's opportunity to nitpick and complain about everything we have done incorrectly. Some supervisors are like that, and if so, here is what you need to do. Never forget to highlight your achievements. You must advocate for yourself. Your review time should never be a time when all your mistakes highlighted. It should be a time to highlight all your strengths, as well as mentioning areas for improvement. If this is not so, ensure that it is. You are not powerless in these sessions, never forget that, and do not sign something that you do not agree with ever!

I also want to add some points when receiving criticism and feedback. It is very natural to be defensive and to be on guard. You cannot listen from the perspective of your emotions. You will react and become reactionary, instead of listening. Listening is essential, and here are a few tips that will help you ensure that you allow yourself to receive the feedback that you need to better yourself.

1. Do not be defensive. Learn to accept constructive criticism. Constructive criticism highlights areas of improvement.

2. Learn to be an active listener – Active listening is when you take the time to fully hear what someone is saying and then having the ability to reiterate what was said. Suppose you cannot do so. Then, you are doing what I call *combative listening*. You have already decided what your response will be. This form of listening is listening to respond. It is not listening because you are taking what someone has said and taking it as a personal attack versus listening and fully understanding the message that the person is attempting to convey.

3. Always ask for examples.

4. Be honest with yourself. You know when specific criticisms apply to you and when they do not. If someone says something and it makes you angry because it hurts your feelings, nine times out of ten, it is something you needed to hear. If you hear something and immediately feel calm, there is a chance that it might not apply to you.

Reflection: Am I aware of my self-worth and my contribution to my job?

47. I Have a Last-Minute Meeting, and I Want to Make a Good Impression

At many points in your professional career, you will receive a last-minute project. It could be leading a meeting, making a formal presentation, or updating others about specific changes that are taking place. You must expect that the last-minute request is going to happen. It is an opportunity for you to make the most of it. It is your time to shine. You must first do your research.

If you are speaking about something unfamiliar to you, take a moment to read up on the topic. Be organized and have hand-outs and other documents ready. Be confident; no one must know that you had five minutes to prepare. You want to demonstrate that you can handle pressure efficiently and effectively. It is your opportunity to shine, so do so.

When it comes to public speaking, it is the one thing that many shy away from and seek to avoid. It is an opportunity for you to showcase unseen talents. You cannot allow shyness, awkwardness, or any insecurities to stand in your way. You must practice what you are going to say, and if you do not have time, you are just going to have to take a deep breath and wing it.

Samuel J. Varner

You will be amazed at how many people simply wing it when it comes to presentations. You are going to have to exude confidence. It is not always easy, but take a deep breath and then know that you can do it. You can do it. If you do not believe that you can, it will show.

Reflection: Do I ensure to the best of my abilities that I maintain an atmosphere of preparedness?

48. If Your Supervisor is About to Jump Ship, Consider Doing the Same

If your supervisor is leaving, find out why. If it is due to a life-changing event or something personal, then that is fine. But if the reason they are resigning is because of looming trouble with the company, then you may want to consider leaving, as well.

A change in management can impact you. A new manager will want to change everything, and change is not always a bad thing, but sometimes, it is not a good thing either. If the new manager is open, attentive, and respects those he/she supervises, then things are okay.

But I also want to mention mass defection. Companies typically have a rotation of departures and new hires. If you are with a company that has a high turnover rate, you need to investigate why the organization has a revolving door. Poorly run companies will state, "Oh, that is just how the industry is." Based on the industry, that statement might have some merit. But overall, there might be some underlying issues.

Companies often fail to manage their greatest resource. The human resource. I am not talking about the Human Resources department. I am talking about the human resource. The wealth of knowledge and expertise that companies fail to utilize. Companies tend to look at an employee based on their job title and not their skills and expertise.

If you notice people are leaving at an alarming rate, it might be time for you to do the same. Overall, pay attention to what is going on around you. You cannot be oblivious to the signs that change is coming. Not all change is adverse. But change can and does affect you. Always be aware of what is going on.

Reflection: Do I keep my eyes and ears open to what is going on around me? Am I aware of the current atmosphere of the organization?

49. Create Your Work Mantra

A mantra is a group of words or phrases that are spoken continuously. It can be a daily affirmation or even a prayer. But I challenge you to make one for yourself. Create one that will inspire you to remain positive despite the external and internal negativity that you may face each day. It does not have to be complicated. It does not have to be a paragraph. Ensure that the mantra fits your needs. I encourage you today to take some time and create one. Consider this a gift to yourself. We must do many things for other people. Rarely, do we take the time to care for ourselves. So, take a moment today and create your mantra. You deserve to be and feel your absolute best every day.

Reflection: What is your mantra to get you through the day?

50. Never Stay Longer than Five Years with a Company if You Have Not Received a Promotion

Time is one of the most precious commodities that we have. Once you have been at a job for many years, it is easy to get comfortable, and with the current state of the economy, looking for another job might seem like a foolish move. The real question is: Are you happy with your job? Are you satisfied with your career path? Are you even on a career path, or do you just have a job? If you are not, and have been feeling that you need a change, let today be the day that you start looking for something better. Or maybe not even better, but a career that speaks to who you are.

One that benefits you and allows you to earn the income that will enable you to live comfortably, but also the flexibility to live and enjoy life. We all deserve to live the lives that we want, but sometimes, we are not willing to do what it takes to obtain that which we most deserve. You do not want to waste your time, energy, and talents if you are not growing career-wise. If this position fits into your career path and it works for you, that is great. We know when it is time to leave. We should not stay longer than we must, which leads to my next rule.

Reflection: Why are you not being promoted? Are you being overlooked?

51. A Job is A Lot Like a Relationship, It Starts Well and Can Go Downhill From There

In the beginning, you get a call saying you received the job. You perform your job with such energy and enthusiasm that you "wow" your supervisor, and your colleagues will start to hate you just a little bit. You give 100% and talk about your job with such joy and glee that your friends begin to consider working for this company. But over time, events occur; sometimes you are in the wrong and sometimes you are not. The thrill is gone. The party is over, and you are unhappy.

If you are unhappy with your job, then it is time to look for another one. The advice that your friends give you about your relationships applies here, as well. Do not stay at a job where you are unhappy. It eats away at your soul. You will become bitter and hate everything and everyone. Look for something else or maybe work in another area—your happiness matters. You cannot perform your job to the best of your abilities when you hate it. You will slowly do enough to get by or to make your boss happy.

You will not go above and beyond. Or you will do things intentionally to strike back at others, everything from missing deadlines to insubordination. No matter what kind of relationship it is, when you act out, you only hurt yourself. The reason you hurt yourself is that you are not operating from an authentic place within yourself. You are reacting off your emotions, and they can change and fade over time. But when you operate from a place of strength, it will not matter about the circumstances. You will act as you always have.

What will give you the courage to do so is the fact that you have a goal in mind. The one thing that will provide you with strength and the ability to persevere through obstacles is when you have a goal in mind.

Reflection: What are your career goals? What do you wish to gain?

52. I'm Getting Fired, All Hope is Not Lost

If you think you are going to be terminated, have a chat with your supervisor or manager. This behavior will demonstrate that you care about your job. It might help you to stave off termination. It is also an opportunity to voice concerns, and sometimes, it can show that there are lapses in management and training. It is a double-edged sword, so be careful with this approach. We are not independently wealthy and need our jobs for daily living. Not only do we have kids that we have to support, but our parents, as well. It is tough out here, and sometimes having a simple conversation can make the difference between maintaining employment or having to file for unemployment.

Here is what you do:

1. If you haven't been arriving on time to work, then show up at least fifteen minutes early every day and when you can stay a little longer to complete tasks, do so.

2. Ask questions, and make sure you are clear about every task. It is up to you to demonstrate that you care about your job.

3. Offer to help others and change your professional image in the workplace, especially if you have a negative one.

4. You cannot afford idle chitchat. Do not linger at anyone's desk. You need to be at your desk working. If you are at someone's desk, you need to pull up a chair and have papers in your hand, because you do not want to appear that you are not working.

5. Take the appropriate amount of time for your lunch break. All those long lunch breaks must stop. At this point, work through your lunch break. You need to show your level of dedication.

6. Silence is golden, and now is the time for you to stop complaining and to stay focused on your work. You do not have time for anything else.

7. Put your cellphone away. Now is not the time to be scrolling through social media.

8. Lastly, do whatever else you can think of that will be beneficial. I do not suggest sleeping with your supervisor.

Reflection: How have you contributed to past, and possibly present, job loss?

53. You Can't Make Everyone Happy, So Don't Even Try

The older you get, you will understand that there will always be someone who does not like you, whether you have given them a good reason or not. You cannot please everyone, and you will only make yourself tired and exhausted if you try to do so. You want your manager to be pleased with your work. You should strive for this if that is currently not the case. But do not confuse that with people-pleasing.

In the office, we must be and should be polite to others. The point that I want to drive home is do not sacrifice your self-worth for others. The more you attempt to please others and seek their approval, the more you tell yourself that you have no value except for the "value" that others place upon you. You will know that all it takes is one situation for people to turn against you. People will sing your praises one moment and stab you in the back the very next.

This rule is about you focusing on your self-esteem and self-worth, and not seeking others to fill a nonexistent void. For when you seek your self-worth from others, internally, you are telling yourself that you are empty and void, and that you need something to fill yourself. But honestly, you are not empty, you have just lost your direction and focus.

I will reiterate one more time. You want your supervisor to be pleased with your work, but if all you want is the approval of others, you are setting yourself up for more disappointment than you realize.

Reflection: Do I seek the approval of others because I tell myself that I am not enough? Do I seek to people-please because I value others more than myself? Do I look for validation in others?

54. My Colleagues Don't Like Me

Well, they might have a good reason. Are you the office snitch or gossip? Are you that person who personifies Dr. Jekyll and Mr. Hyde? Are you cheerful and sunny one day and the next hostile, and non-communicative? Does your mood depend solely on your emotional state? If the answer is yes to any of these questions, chances are, you are the problem and not everyone else.

If you hate everyone in your office or a good majority, you could be the problem. Maybe you talk too much or are the first to spread any gossip. Perhaps, you share your opinion when no one has asked for it. Remember, it is a job, and not a popularity contest; well, not entirely. However, people who like you, help you. People who do not like you will do everything to see you transferred, demoted, or fired. They do not care which one, as long as something unfortunate happens to you.

By the way, everyone will not like you. It is one notion you need to release. You should strive to get along with everyone. If you do not get along with anyone, you are the problem, and you need to fix it.

Reflection: Have I fostered a positive work environment where my colleagues feel comfortable to engage me, or do I contribute to the negative work environment perpetuated by others?

55. Gossip is Not Necessarily a Bad Thing, but Always Beware of the Office Gossiper

It is a tricky rule because gossip can have some thread of validity depending upon the source. It is your job not to spread gossip, but only information. If you hear something, do not run and tell someone else. It could be a trick depending upon the person. Also, you could be spreading false information, which can make you look like a troublemaker, and that is not the image you want to portray. If you are a troublemaker, and then continue down your path, you will only cause trouble for yourself. It is only a matter of time.

We want to know more about our colleagues, especially if they are interesting people. However, it is not your responsibility to ensure that everyone knows everything about another person. Gossiping in the office has led to altercations, dislikes, and even termination of employment. The office gossip is someone who wishes to ensure that drama occurs within the office. They are not happy unless something is going on. These colleagues will want to know your opinion about everything.

Always remain vague, and you will avoid their trap. Now, they will be willing to tell you many things that I would advise, not repeating. If you go back and tell others, you are part of the network and playing directly into their hands.

Samuel J. Varner

Reflection: Am I the office gossip? Am I responsible for some of the discord around me?

56. Sometimes, Your Colleagues are the Real Face of Evil

Colleagues are an unusual breed of people. It is essential to understand that work is not a social event, and no one is there for social reasons. People work because they need money for the necessities and pleasures that life has to offer. It is important to remember this. If a situation arises that could result in termination, remember your colleagues will look out for themselves and not for you, especially if they have others who depend on their income. With that in mind, let's look at the basic personality types of colleagues.

The first one is someone I call *the pleaser*. This colleague seeks to make everyone happy. They always want to smooth out rough situations, and they want everyone to get along and to be satisfied. These colleagues can be kind people, but they can also be manipulative. You see, they are willing to make anyone and everyone happy. They will do so at your expense. While they are talking to you, they are also talking to others. Pleasers rarely share their true feelings, and will oftentimes agree with the group, even though they disagree. If you are around them long enough, you will see through their façade and trust me; you will not like what you see.

The second are people I call *hostiles*. I call them hostiles because they are hostile about every idea, every thought, and do not like anyone. I will not say avoid these types of colleagues, but they move with the waves of their emotions. They will speak to you one day and then not talk to you the next day. Exercise caution because these types of colleagues make everyone the enemy, and they will one day make you the enemy.

The third are ones I call *the barely-enough*. These are the colleagues who get on your last nerve because they do just barely enough work, but want praise for every little average thing that they do. They tend to complain about everything. They tend to bring down morale, and they often want you to join in. I would advise against it. They are also the types who are likely to take credit for your work. Do not trust these type of colleagues.

The fourth type is the *private colleagues*. The private colleagues are polite, can be silent, and do not ask anything of anyone unless they need it. These types of colleagues are sometimes jaded. These individuals tend to do their work. They come in on time and leave on time, and try not to cause trouble. These are the colleagues you want as allies. They will help you out when you need it. They will also give you good advice.

The fifth type is the *social butterfly*. They love to speak to everyone. You will always see them in someone else's cubicle or the hallways. When they are not working, they are striking up a conversation with someone. While these people can be kind and caring, they can also have diarrhea of the mouth.

Developing the Workforce of YOU!

The last type I will call *haters*. They are similar to hostiles, but these colleagues are not happy unless someone is angry with someone. These types of colleagues will tell you something that someone else said about you without you asking for information. They can and will share this information with you, so you do not like another. They cause tension for various reasons, and have an unhappy work life, home life to honestly just being a nasty person.

Now, remember it is easy to point fingers and say I am not a *hostile*, or a *barely-enough*, or a *hater*. But let's be honest, at some point or another, we all have exhibited these types of behaviors, and they are not conducive to the productive work environment. You must identify these colleagues who closely mimic these types of behaviors, but be honest with yourself about which personality type you are. Not all of the types mentioned are necessarily bad, but they are not necessarily good either. Creating a balance is suggested.

Reflection: What type of person are you? Be honest with yourself?

57. Do Not Expect to Always Get Along with Your Supervisor

Expect that sometimes they will rub you the wrong way, irritate you, and that they will dislike you first before you can dislike them. Dealings with your supervisor will not be smooth. They can be stressful, challenging, and exhausting. You can survive and thrive if you play your cards right. Not all supervisors or managers are bad. Honestly, most are ill-trained and ill-suited for managing others. Most are honestly pushed through the ranks as the company has expanded or have positioned themselves as opportunities have become available. A manager is only as good as the training that they receive and their personality. Personality tends to win.

Take a moment to understand your supervisor. Is he/she overworked, stressed, and pulled in many directions? If so, offer to assist them with their work. You want to be known as helpful. It can also backfire because you do not want to end up doing your supervisor's job.

It is your responsibility to understand your supervisor's personality. It is up to you to create a harmonious working relationship with them and not the other way around. I know that some people will disagree, but here is why. You want to eliminate as much stress as possible from your work life.

The best way to do so is to understand them as a person. They will respect you and like you because they will see that you took the time to understand them as a person. They might not necessarily like you, but they will know that when they speak to you, you will understand them.

Reflection: How do you ensure that you maintain healthy communication with your supervisor?

58. My Colleagues Perform the Same Job I Do and Make More than Me

It has happened to me, and I have seen it happen to others, as well. Your job duties are strikingly similar, if not the same, as your colleagues. There will be times that you will find out someone's pay. No one has violated any HR rules, but sometimes, you just happen to see something, or the other person states their salary. Your initial reaction will be anger. You will be angry because your feelings are hurt.

In our eyes, a person who makes more is valued more within the company. You do not go around the office telling everyone that your colleagues earn more than you. You do not begin a vicious smear campaign to make them look bad, so you have a better chance of a promotion. You do not start to have a slack work ethic. You do the complete opposite.

Should you have a discussion with your manager about the difference in pay? I would advise against it. Here is why. Your manager will inquire about how you obtained this knowledge. Also, your approach could be off-putting and could end up having an unfavorable outcome.

There is a new trend that some companies are beginning to follow. Most companies do not disclose pay, but there are companies now that are beginning to list salary ranges. Advocates for this believe that by doing so, instances of discrimination concerning compensation will decrease and that companies can demonstrate that salaries are comparable with the industry. Some see this to boost morale. Since with transparency, there are no secret wages.

The rationale is simple: two people who perform the same job should receive equal pay, and if compensation is transparent, then it will promote equality.

Reflection: What do you think? Do you agree or disagree? Would you want your position and pay rate to be public knowledge?

59. Take the Time to Foster Positive Relationships Within Your Department and Companywide

You must foster positive working relationships with your colleagues. You must ensure to the best of your abilities that you get along. You do not want to make enemies with your colleagues. We all know that everyone will not like us, but that does not mean that you give other's reasons to dislike you. You want to foster positive relationships with your colleagues because, at some point, you are going to need them.

Trust me; it is better when people like and respect you than when people hate you. There will be times where you will need advice, and you will need historical knowledge that they can give. Do not cut yourself short and remember, every work relationship can and does have some value.

Also, do not neglect to associate with people outside of your department. They can also be a wealth of knowledge. Your goal is to gain as much knowledge as possible. You are an asset to the organization, and you want to be regarded as such. Respect your professional relationships. That will mean putting your attitude aside and treating others better than you usually do.

Samuel J. Varner

Reflection: How do I treat the people I work with daily? Have I done everything possible to foster a positive working relationship with them?

60. Cultural Biases Can Hinder Your Growth

Pay attention to the demographics within a department. We have all seen it. Look at the various departments within your organization. Are they predominately one ethnicity? It is our human nature to gravitate to those who are most like us, and sometimes with companies and hiring practices, you will see this happen. It is not the end of the world, but be aware. I wish I could say that racism, nepotism, and all of the other *isms* out there did not exist. But the truth of the matter is that they do.

Do not let this stop you or deter you from your dreams. Always pay attention to the things around you and have an air of suspicion about certain things. It helps always to keep an open mind. The saying goes: "Things are not always as they seem." It is true, but sometimes things are exactly the way we see them. We just choose to ignore what we see.

Reflection: Take a moment to look at the different departments in your organization? What do you see? What don't you see?

61. My Job is Secure

No, it is not, and do not ever believe that lie. Everyone from the janitor to CEO's have been fired or laid-off. I have seen this time and time again. Colleagues develop relationships with Senior Management or ensure that they are the only knowledge base to guarantee their longevity, and that works for a time. But all things must come to an end. No matter how long you have been with the company, no matter who you know or what you have accomplished, you are not untouchable. You should never think that, and to do so is ludicrous.

All it takes is one incident or several, and you can be out the door. Never become too comfortable, too complacent, in your position and understand that at any given point and time, anyone can be replaced.

The best way to secure your job is to make yourself invaluable and be known for having the right positive attitude and work ethic. People will remember you and look out for you. It is what you want. You want people to think of you in a positive light. Because when opportunities arise, they will think of you. This ties in with how you treat others and your level of professionalism.

Reflection: How do you make yourself invaluable? Do you do all that you can to ensure you job ethically?

62. Laugh as Much as You Can in the Office, but Don't Make it a Party

I know I have given so many rules and have used the words *don't* and *never* more than you want to hear. But here is one rule you will like. Your colleagues aren't all evil. They also like to laugh and have fun. From time to time, we all need to laugh. We need to build positive bonds with those that we work with, so laugh and enjoy the day as much as possible. Get your work done, but do not forget to laugh and share positive and fun times with your colleagues. Life is hard and stressful, and laughter is good for the soul.

It is up to you to foster a positive work environment. It is your responsibility to create a positive atmosphere. I know that your colleagues may have wronged you, and you may have wronged them. But at the end of the day, it is about you and your happiness. Forgive them and let it go. You cannot and should not hold onto past transgressions. It will only make you miserable.

Reflection: What am I doing to create and foster a more positive and healthy work environment?

63. Organizational Culture, Every Company is Unique

You must look at each organization as if it is a person. It has its own unique set of morals, ethics, and personality. Some companies are strict about their dress code, and some allow for dress down days. Some have flexible work schedules, and some are very rigid when it comes to your work schedule. Be noticeably clear and aware of the culture of the organization.

Organizational Culture comprises the values, culture, and the morals that the company subscribes to. Culture varies on the type of entity and the leadership at the time. Here is what you need to know. Some companies focus on education, diversity, self-empowerment, …etc. The list can go on. If you understand your company's organizational culture, you will understand how the company can truly benefit you.

Reflection: Are you aware of the culture of your current job? Does that culture fit you?

64. "Isms" in the Office

Some people wish to believe that racism and injustice do not exist. For the rest of us who live in the real world, we must understand and accept that sexism, racism, and discrimination do exist. If you are experiencing any form of discrimination, you must report it. If you sit in silence and say, "That's just how things are here." Then, unfortunately, you are part of the problem. It takes a great deal of courage to face these issues head-on. Many have lost their jobs and even their careers.

Speaking up has a price but so, too, does silence. It is easy to say you need to speak up. But if you are the sole supporter of your family and you fear retaliation, then it is easier said than done. The point I want to make is that we do not live in a perfect world. Some people will judge you because you are not like them. Or they will believe that a man is better and can do a better job than a woman. You must always be clear about these things and then, challenge the status quo and help to effect change. It is not easy. It is never easy when you confront injustice.

Reflection: Are you an advocate for others?

65. Never Work with Friends, Well Sometimes

If you go into business with your friends, heed the following:

1. Have clear expectations and roles.

2. Know your friend's strengths and weaknesses. It is not an opportunity to lie to yourself, be clear.

3. Have an exit plan. Things can go sour, or a couple of life hiccups, and your friends may not be trustworthy. Always have an executable and viable exit plan.

If you work for the same company, the same department, then:

1. Know that people will hate you for this relationship.

2. If one of you becomes a supervisor, prepare for the hatred and backlash from your colleagues that will ensue.

3. If the friendship goes sour, be prepared for all your business to be shared with everyone.

4. If your friend has a horrible reputation, remember these words: "Birds of a feather, flock together."

In my honest opinion, if you are going into business together, give it a lot of thought.

Reflection: Are you prepared for your work-life and personal life to overlap in ways that you might not be comfortable with?

66. Never Work with Your Spouse, Personal & Work-Life Will Become One

I say never, but it happens. You can meet at work or you both can start a business together. It is not a bad thing; however, you must do what is necessary to make things comfortable for you and your spouse. If you work for the same company, here are some rules:

1. Do not go to lunch together all the time. It hinders you from getting to know your colleagues and to form meaningful working relationships.

2. If you don't have a hobby, you need one. Couples who spend too much of their time together tend to have space issues. They tend to feel crowded. You must have that one thing that you do alone. They say, "Absence makes the heart grow fonder." In this case, I agree.

3. Do not be affectionate in the office, everyone will know that you are together, but it will make some people feel uncomfortable to see open and sometimes explicit displays of affection.

If you start a business together, here are some tips:

1. Be clear about each other's roles and define duties.

2. Be sure your relationship can handle spending all your time together.

3. Encourage your partner to spend some time away from the business and to enjoy time with friends and family.

4. There will be times when you will disagree, but remember, you are not enemies; you are working towards the same goals.

Reflection: Are you prepared for a complicated life where work and personal are not one?

67. Never Work with Siblings, They Will Expect You to Do it All, While They Do Nothing

We know our siblings. We all know that one who is the overachiever, then one we know that will get the job done. We all know that one who will get nothing done. You need to remember that when working with family, it is one of the toughest jobs in the world. You have to find a balance between your personal life and your work life, and the two will often cross and become tangled. If you can avoid it, do.

Stand up for yourself and call your siblings out when necessary. Be honest and real about what will happen and ask yourself if this is the career path that you want. I advise never to work with them. If it is unavoidable, then do everything it takes to make it work. Identify problems and later try to resolve them. You might be the problem, and if so, then you must become the solution.

Reflection: Does it make sense to work with your siblings?

68. Office Relationships-Beware

Office romances happen. There is nothing that can be said or done to make them disappear. If there are two people in proximity to each other that share mutual feelings, something is bound to happen. Nine times out of ten, these relationships end in disaster, and if the other person is your supervisor, then beware. I advise against it, but you will just do it anyway, so here is my advice.

Now concerning dating, it is important to remember that dating a colleague in your department is something you should probably never do. If the relationship goes sour, be prepared for backlash and retaliation. If this person works for the company but is in another department, remember discretion is essential.

Do not send e-mails to each other during work. Do not have lunch together too often. Do not tell anyone at work, and above all, make sure that this person is someone you want to establish a relationship with and not someone you are solely attracted to sexually. Relationships with colleagues rarely work out and often cause added stress and more uncomfortable situations.

Some companies have strict policies about office romance. It is good to know your company's policies before engaging in any form of a relationship (including a drunken one-night stand). These can be disastrous for your career and can have negative implications for years to come.

My advice is not to entertain these types of relationships. Often, disaster is looming, but there have been instances where people met at the office and fall in love. It can happen. Usually, it just ends badly, and there is a lot of gossip.

Reflection: Are you aware of the ramifications that office romance can cause?

69. Family-Owned Businesses are a Double-Edged Sword

There are benefits to working in a family-owned business. It is excellent for those who are entry-level and need experience. You will learn a great deal about the company. Your role will incorporate more than just your duties, and you will get to see what it takes to run a business. There are some downfalls, and one of them is pay. Often, only the owners make the real money.

If you are looking to climb the corporate ladder, then a family-owned business is not right for you. Depending upon the type of company and size, you might be able to advance and earn a decent salary. No two companies are exactly alike, but only when you know what your goals are, can you decide if an employer fits your needs.

Reflection: Is this environment conducive to my career goals and personal job growth?

70. My Boss is an Idiot

Okay, well, that might be true. We all believe that we can do things better than someone else, especially our supervisors. However, it is to your advantage to create a symbiotic relationship with your supervisor that promotes mutual benefit. It is not easy, and ego can get in the way, but if you can accomplish this, it should make your work life a little easier. I will admit, I have never been a supervisor. It is easy to say this. I have. But one thing you must understand is that your supervisor has roles and responsibilities that you do not have. If you are not managing someone or do not have supervisory duties, you cannot fully understand the amount of pressure that they deal with on any given day.

Your accidental screw up can be their nightmare and can create problems for your entire team. Your supervisor might not be an idiot, but their focus is not the same as yours. Always remember that. But they could also be an idiot. I know that you have some stories. We all do. But remember, we all can be, at times. Since we all have been and acted like one from time to time, we must help our fellow *idiots*.

Reflection: Have I taken an opportunity to understand the role and daily pressures that my supervisor must endure? Do I make his/her job less stressful?

71. My Boss Thinks He/She Knows Everything

Do not argue with or challenge your supervisor. They will always be "right," and you will still be wrong, even when evidence points to the contrary. They are trying to secure their position. Always remain calm. Appropriately offer your thoughts and watch this supervisor end up going with the route that you suggested. They have hopes, dreams, and fears of inadequacy. Cut them some slack sometimes; we all need it every so often.

Sometimes, you need to admit that you can be a "know-it-all," as well. You can act, say, and do things that will give others the same perception. We often emulate this. It is in our nature to seek revenge and vengeance for all grievances, both small and significant. We do not face our pain but instead, pass it along to others. You might not want to admit it, but sometimes, when you are having a bad day, you feel better when you make someone else feel the same way.

We often transfer our energy and emotions to another to alleviate any feelings and pain that we experience, instead of facing and confronting it head-on. Challenge yourself not to shift your negativity to others. We all know the saying about *karma*, but we do not like to own up that sometimes, when something comes to us, it is because we sent it out in the first place.

Reflection: What are you doing to manage your supervisor?

72. Don't be Condescending

As a supervisor, you set the tone for your team. I have encountered many a supervisor who has acted as if they were a supreme ruler or God Himself. Their word is law, and everything that they do is above reproach and questioning. Empires fall, and you are not the exception to the rule. When you manage others, you have responsibilities. One responsibility is respect. You do have the right to mistreat, demean, or humiliate others. You do not have the right to use language or tone to make them feel less than. If you do this, you are abusive.

Abuse does not have to be physical; it can be verbal, as well. Intimidation is also a form of abuse. You must ask yourself this one important question. Do I want to be respected or feared? When people respect you, even if they disagree with you, they will be willing to work with you. People will only be afraid for a while before they resist it. Fear has an expiration date. At some point, they will be tired of being scared, and they will fight back. It would be something you do not want, especially if you attacked everyone around you. My enemy's enemy is my friend.

No one is perfect, and we all make mistakes, but there comes a point in time that we know what we are doing. What you give out, you will get back in return, so what do you want in return: respect or fear?

If this applies to you, here is what you do. You put yourself in the other person's shoes. Put your sarcasm away. Think before you speak. Use words that encourage others and promote respect. It is not always what you say, but how you say it. You do not have to call someone *stupid* to call them stupid. You do not have to tell everyone that you think you are better than them to do so. Your actions speak loudly.

Reflection: How do I communicate with those whom I supervise? Do I create an open environment for creativity and constructive criticism, or is my management style more of a dictatorship?

73. Your Boss's Boss is an Excellent Person to Get to Know

You need leverage in the office. It's a jungle. While it doesn't secure your job forever, it can make your job a little easier. At a previous job, I went to lunch with my supervisor's supervisor. It was a mentorship lunch. I wanted to advance, and honestly, I needed the guidance. I knew how my supervisor was, and I wanted to keep it a secret. I knew that jealousy would occur. I just wanted to advance myself and grow.

My supervisor found out and turned on me. I became public enemy number one, but after a while, she became afraid of me. I would talk with her boss often about mentorship and how I could succeed in a career path, but this made her treat me differently. I saw that she had a bit of fear when it came to me.

You must position yourself and take full advantage of the opportunities. If you want to move into management, then you need someone to mentor you. Mentorship is vitally crucial for career growth. You must always invest in yourself.

Reflection: Am I networking within my organization? Am I forming professional relationships with people who can help me advance within the company?

74. If Your Supervisor Doesn't Like You, then Quit or Find Another Job ASAP!

Everyone will not like you, and this applies to your supervisor, as well. They manage you and are responsible for every mistake that you make. Of course, you are accountable, but their manager will hold them accountable for everything wrong that you do. It is essential to understand the difference between your supervisor expecting the best from you versus your supervisor being out to get you. Your perception of your supervisor will dictate your actions. Your actions based on opinions can cause you trouble. For example, your supervisor states the following:

"I've noticed that your work performance is below average, and I need you to remain focused on your work and not to be distracted."

The tone of these words and the body language will dictate how you receive this message, along with your perceptions and views. While the statement above might not possess derogatory language, you can interpret the statement to mean that the supervisor is saying you are doing everything but your work. You spend too much time doing other things.

If your supervisor makes enough of these statements or criticizes everything that you do, whether good, bad, or indifferent, it might be time for you to look for another job, and here is why. If your current work environment is not conducive to your job growth, you should not remain there. If you are receiving criticisms but not constructive feedback, you will not grow. You will feel inept, and sometimes your supervisor will want you to feel this way, especially if he/she does not care for you. No work environment is perfect; no manger is perfect; no person is perfect. However, we all know when we have a work environment that brings out the best in us and one that tears us down.

However, if you have a supervisor who consistently brings you down, who is negative about everything that you do and shoots down every idea with a rocket launcher, then it is time to leave. You cannot grow and be your best if the environment is not suited for you to grow. It is like placing a seed on a rock and hoping that it will grow into a healthy tree, but without giving it the nutrients it needs to grow.

Reflection: How do I take criticism? Have I learned to differentiate between constructive and destructive criticism?

75. Help! My Boss Takes Credit for My Work

I am sorry to say that this happens all the time. I will not say that there is nothing that you can do. You are your greatest cheerleader. Do not let an opportunity pass you by, where you can let others know that you worked on this project with your supervisor. You will have to be creative in doing so. You do not want to appear to brag, but you also do not want to make your supervisor look like a thief, even though that might be the case. It is crucial to receive credit for the work that you do. You will have to be creative to ensure that others know of the work that you do.

Reflection: How can I ensure that I receive credit for my work?

76. Keep a Work Journal, It's More Important than You Think

It is the one rule that no one tells you. You come to work every day. You perform the tasks given to you, and then you go home. We all know that this is far from true. We all know that there are all sorts of drama that ensues throughout the day. Unfortunately, there will be incidents that you will need to record. There will be situations that will need to involve HR, EEO, and other groups. It is important to have all your facts straight. You need to make sure you include the following:

1. The date of the incident.
2. The parties present.
3. What occurred (truthfully).
4. Actions that were taken against you after said incident.

No one wants to go through the bother of doing this. It is hard to do so, but there will come a time when having a work journal is essential. We would all like to believe that everyone treats others fairly all the time, but that is not the case. There are all sorts of *isms* in the world, and discrimination and sexual harassment occur more often than is reported.

You can keep your work journal in a pad at your desk. However, I would advise against that. Electronic format is best, but keep paper copies someplace safe. Do not disclose to anyone that you have a work journal. Others will want to pry and see what is inside of it. Someone might just attempt to steal it.

Reflection: Do you have a work journal?

77. Sexual Harassment

It is something that no one wants to talk about. It is something that companies wish to avoid. It is something that you cannot ignore. Sexual harassment is making unwelcomed or inappropriate advances of a sexual nature. Sexual harassment is more complicated in scope. There are many layers, and your character will come into question, especially if you are the party that is receiving the harassment. Harassment must be proven. You must report it right away. You will receive unwanted scrutiny into your character and personal life.

Sexual harassment is about power and using said power to influence others in an unprofessional manner. You must document every e-mail, every conversation, and everything that will show proof that harassment is taking place. The burden of proof lies with you.

Do not forget to talk to a professional about this situation. This situation will take an emotional toll on you, and it is best to obtain the tools to deal with it. It is traumatic for any person who is being harassed, and it is best to get the help you need. I also want to mention that men can be harassed, as well.

Be mindful of what you say to others. Compliments are allowed, but even then, you must be mindful of what you say and how you say it. You can say something that, to you, is completely harmless, but to another, can be misconstrued as harassment. You must think about what you say and how you say it. Everyone is not your friend, and sometimes, people are looking to take anything and everything you say and use it against you.

Reflection: Are you ready to stand up for yourself and others?

78. Always Leave with Dignity & Respect

No matter the situation, whether you are fired, laid-off, or resigned, do not show any emotions. All three can be an emotional experience. If you are fired, just take your things and leave. Nowadays, you are often escorted out by security. Do not make a scene; it only makes you look bad. It's humiliating enough to be escorted out. Hold your head up high and leave with the same dignity and respect that you came with on your first day. If you are laid-off, do the same as above.

Some companies will remove you from the premises immediately, or some will let you work up until a specific time. If this is the case, then you show your professionalism and ensure that projects are completed. You should also do this when you resign. You do not owe anyone anything, but you want your reputation to be intact. You always want to make sure that you present yourself in the most professional light. You might come across these same people again in your professional career.

Reflection: Do you carry yourself with dignity even during tough times and situations?

79. You Will Know When It's Time to Leave

It is a feeling or a confirmation. It is something that you will just know. There will not be any rhyme or reason or scientific method. You will know. Begin looking, but do not tell anyone and do not broadcast it. Just take time to look for something that is along the lines of what you want to do. If you are not sure yet, think of all the things that you do not want to do. It will guide you towards that which you do want to do.

It will be hard to leave your current employer because you will make some great connections with people, and you will feel a sense of duty and obligation to the company. Those feelings are entirely natural. The longer you have been on your job, the stronger your sense of responsibility and commitment will be. However, your highest sense of duty and obligation is to yourself and no one else.

It is time to update your resume and reach out to your professional connections to gain perspective and direction. Do not jump from one dead-end job to another, unless you believe that you will be either fired or laid-off. Then, you will want to jump ship as soon as possible. If that is not the case, then take your time until you are clear about what you want. Always be clear about what you want.

Reflection: Is it time to look for another job or embark on a new career path?

80. It's Only a Job

At the end of the day, when you have locked your computer, put on your coat, and said good night, the workday is over, and tomorrow will be another day. Our jobs are what we do to sustain ourselves. Some of us must hold down multiple jobs to sustain ourselves. It is only a job. Don't make it your life! If you do, when it ends, you will feel empty, broken, and that your life has no value because you made this job the source of your self-worth and validation. A job cannot validate you just like standing in a parking garage cannot make you a car. You are your source, and you validate your existence, nothing and no one else can.

The most important "things" in your life are your friends and family. Jobs will come and go. You can get another job, but you cannot replace a person who is near and dear to your heart. Yes, it is important to have a job. But it is also important to spend time with friends and family. Make sure that you spend time with them, or you will have a lifetime of regret. Do not forget about yourself. Do not forget to do the things that make you happy along the way. You are important. That is the reason I wrote this book. I want you to remember that your existence matters, and nothing or no one should ever be your source.

Again, it is only a job. Do the best that you can. Give it your all, but not your essence. You save that for yourself and those in your life whom you love.

Reflection: Are you aware of what this job truly is with respect to your life and existence? Are you aware that it is part of your journey and not your life?

ABOUT THE AUTHOR

My name is Samuel Varner. I possess an MBA with a concentration in Finance from Strayer University, located in Washington, DC. At the age of 19, I gave my first financial talk. Personal finance, investing, and business have always been a passion of mine. After many years of learning, research, and providing sound professional advice, I have decided to pursue this endeavor of education.

As I have journeyed through my professional career and have had more downs than ups, I have learned a great deal about others but more importantly, myself. We lack the necessary tools to navigate life, let alone the office. This book is a compilation of my trials, errors, and wisdom gained.

As a person, I want to see others succeed. I want to see others achieve their absolute best and my mission is to support others not only in their financial journey, but in their professional journey, as well.

www.ingramcontent.com/pod-product-compliance
Lightning Source LLC
Chambersburg PA
CBHW060835220526
45466CB00003B/1118